URBAN PIONEER

URBAN PIONEER

INTERIORS INSPIRED BY INDUSTRIAL DESIGN

SARA EMSLIE

Photography by
BENJAMIN EDWARDS

RYLAND PETERS & SMALL
LONDON • NEW YORK

Senior designer Toni Kay
Senior commissioning editor
 Annabel Morgan
Location research Sara Emslie
 and Jess Walton
Production manager
 Patricia Harrington
Art director Leslie Harrington
Editorial director Julia Charles
Publisher Cindy Richards

First published in 2017 by
Ryland Peters & Small
20–21 Jockey's Fields,
London WC1R 4BW
and
341 East 116th Street
New York, NY 10029

www.rylandpeters.com

Text copyright © Sara Emslie 2017
Design and photographs copyright
© Ryland Peters & Small 2017

10 9 8 7 6 5 4 3 2 1

ISBN 978-1-84975-800-0

A CIP record for this book is available
from the British Library.

Library of Congress CIP data has been
applied for.

Printed and bound in China

CONTENTS

WHAT IS AN URBAN PIONEER?

Urban Pioneering is about championing the best of ex-industrial spaces and the products designed to be used within them to create unique homes with a distinctive aesthetic. This book visits a selection of such properties and meets the people who have transformed them into unique spaces that both retain their architectural integrity and meet the practical needs of their inhabitants.

The first conversions of factories and warehouses to residential spaces took place in the 1950s and '60s. A decline in manufacturing meant that many inner-city industrial buildings became vacant, attracting the first wave of urban pioneers – artists seeking cheap rents and large interiors to use as studio spaces. Since then, ex-industrial areas in many cities have become sought-after residential districts and the trend shows no sign of abating, with a second generation of urban pioneers now converting warehouses, schools, factories, pubs, offices and retail spaces into inspired modern homes.

Former industrial buildings tend to share a distinctive aesthetic. Structural elements play a starring role, huge windows allow the light to flood in and expansive floorplans allow for open-plan living. Brickwork is left exposed and original wooden floors remain resolutely unpolished. This industrial look has, in turn, led to the increased popularity of industrial designs that were originally created for use in factories and other workspaces – task lighting, station clocks, hospital beds, cast-iron radiators and factory stools. Thanks to their no-nonsense, utilitarian styling, such products are now sought-after style statements, whether they are vintage pieces or modern interpretations of original designs. Of course, such pieces work perfectly in ex-industrial spaces, but they also have the capacity to transform a comfortable but architecturally undistinguished interior, such as a new build, into a unique living space with a sense of history and a personality of its own.

URBAN DESIGN AND STYLE

URBAN DESIGN

REMODELLING AN INDUSTRIAL SPACE INTO A RESIDENTIAL ONE can be time-consuming, costly and fraught with problems. However, for individuals undeterred by the potential difficulties, and for architects and interior designers who thrive on the challenge of injecting new life into a neglected or abandoned space, the final results can be inspiring. The key is finding the space that is right for you.

INDUSTRIAL SPACES

The lofts and warehouses built by merchants and traders during the 18th and 19th centuries and the factories and textile mills constructed during the Industrial Revolution represent commercial spaces at perhaps their most formidable. Often vast in scale and with a wealth of architectural features, these former bastions of industry are coveted by those who want to create a unique living space with decorative flair.

Buying a home in a building that has already been converted by a developer means that you can enjoy the spirit of the building and the original aesthetic without having to undertake any of the more complicated and prolonged architectural and construction processes. And as many larger spaces are reconfigured and sectioned up into individual units, they provide a ready-made community too.

OPPOSITE LEFT Warehouses, factories and commercial buildings that were once symbols of prosperous economic times have been abandoned and allowed to fall into a state of decay and disrepair in many modern post-industrial economies. On the waterfront in Brooklyn, New York, nature has taken hold of a building that is ripe for redevelopment.

OPPOSITE RIGHT Cast-iron fire escapes dominate the facades of so many American warehouses and factories. Built to satisfy new safety laws introduced in the early 20th century, they are considered by many to be desirable architectural features worth the considerable renovation sums involved.

BELOW LEFT The classic features we associate with industrial buildings were originally introduced for practical purposes. Robust metal was used for everything from railings and staircases to chain-link fences and window frames. For modern developers seeking an industrial aesthetic, it is worth restoring original metalwork that has rusted or disintegrated over time.

BOTTOM LEFT Redundant commercial buildings such as former garages, storage units or boarded-up retail premises exist as pockets of potential throughout our towns and cities.

BELOW Industrial buildings that are considered to be of historical or architectural significance may have restrictions with regards to any modifications. Restoring original features to their former glory, such as these magnificent doors to a 17th-century Amsterdam warehouse, is crucial for a successful renovation.

THIS PAGE Preserving original features can result in a unique interior full of authentic factory chic. Concrete support columns, exposed piping and steel windows create a dramatic look in this cavernous former manufacturing space. The building's history was celebrated by retaining the peeling paint and the rusting metal windows rather than replacing them. The original ceiling-mounted pipework has been painted bright red to become a distinctive decorative feature.

FAR LEFT Builder's numbers painted on a wall during construction work are a quirky, eye-catching detail and provide the finished interior with a memento of its transformation from a commercial site into a domestic one. Crumbling plaster and exposed brickwork also add character to the end result.

LEFT Tin ceiling tiles were originally produced as a functional and affordable alternative to decorative plasterwork and were widely installed in American warehouses and workplaces. Vintage originals can be sourced and make an authentic design feature in an industrial-style interior, although they must be expertly restored if covered in lead paint.

BELOW Blending obtrusive industrial features such as a heavy metal door and frame into a minimal living space is easily achieved with a unifying coat of paint. White is ideal, as it is pared-down and utilitarian in style, and widely used in both commercial and domestic interiors.

Committed urban pioneers wanting to plough their own furrow, however, could consider a factory or warehouse that is still unconverted. While taking on such a large commitment requires serious financial outlay, the potential to stamp your own style on such a building is enormous.

Old civic or municipal buildings such as schools and hospitals offer rich opportunities for redevelopment. Find one in its original state and you are likely to stumble upon a treasure trove of utilitarian features. Built to last, with large windows, high ceilings, cast-iron radiators and wood block flooring, such premises can be transformed into bright and airy interiors.

As urban areas become increasingly built up and developed, finding a space to convert requires creative thinking and an element of compromise. Garages, small factories and commercial sites all have potential for transformation into unique contemporary homes, but bear in mind that

LEFT Industrial materials are suitably heavy duty, tough and robust. In an old naval canteen, steel joists and sheets of plywood create an authentic urban look. The polished concrete floor is hardwearing, easy to clean and only gets more attractive with age. Factor one in at the design stage so that it can be combined with underfloor heating for practicality and comfort.

OPPOSITE ABOVE Metal-framed glass screens and partitions are ideal for dividing spaces without reducing the amount of available natural light. Wire-mesh glass is reminiscent of old industrial buildings where a grid of wire was incorporated into the glass to prevent it from shattering in the event of fire. Today it is more widely used to create a hardworking utilitarian style in interior design.

OPPOSITE BELOW LEFT Features typical of factories and warehouses, such as exposed plumbing pipes and stopcocks, are worth retaining if at all possible, especially as wall-mounted pipes and wiring also make for easy maintenance. Entire heating and plumbing systems can be overhauled or reconditioned for modern living standards if required, although the work may be costly.

OPPOSITE BELOW RIGHT Urban pioneers are adept at embracing the beauty in the ordinary. The plumbing pipes and plastic tubing under this kitchen sink have been left on show and provide a dash of utilitarian chic. For further visual impact, scaffolding poles and reclaimed timber boards have been repurposed into a unit for the basin to sit on.

planning permission will be required for any additions or extensions that increase the size of the building. Original features such as vintage signage or retail fittings are often found in old commercial spaces and can be factored into a renovation to add quirky charm.

GETTING STARTED

Anyone wanting to develop an ex-commercial or industrial building will need to apply for permission for change of use to residential. This isn't always automatically granted, and can present a major hurdle. If the building is listed or considered to be of historical significance, then consent will be required for any changes or modifications to the exterior or interior. For complex renovations, an experienced architect and contractor is essential if you are to both realize your vision and adhere to building regulations.

For the best results, work with what you have rather than against it and be sympathetic when restoring original features. Retain anything that creates a record of the building's former use, as it will add authenticity to the final result. Make sure any materials that don't satisfy today's health and safety standards (such as lead paint or asbestos tiles) are removed by professionals.

Plan your internal space before you start the renovation. Large warehouses are generally too large to make a single dwelling and need to be subdivided into loft-style apartments. High ceilings offer the possibility of mezzanine levels, while open-plan spaces can be divided up into smaller spaces with partitions, walls or pod-like structures. Many industrial buildings have huge windows to make the most of the natural light. These areas are ideal for kitchens and living zones,

whereas bathrooms and bedrooms can be tucked away behind full-height or mid-height internal walls.

Smaller ex-commercial spaces such as garages or retail units are also likely to require reconfiguration and perhaps the addition of extra floors or a basement level, subject to planning consent. Do consider upside-down living, where the bedrooms are on the lower level with living and sociable spaces upstairs, if this makes the most of any striking architectural features.

BREATHING NEW LIFE INTO OLD

The raw fabric and bare bones of a building's structure are what provides an industrial conversion with character and soul. Embrace imperfections, ensuring they aren't covered up during renovation works. Exposed brickwork can be preserved and protected with a clear varnish. Concrete beamed walls and ceilings exude industrial appeal if left uncovered, as do concrete floors. Original tiles can be restored and any gaps filled with replacements sourced from specialist suppliers or salvage merchants.

Architectural fixtures and fittings that are remnants of the building's history are also worth retaining.

OPPOSITE BELOW LEFT Dividers and screens are ideal for sectioning off space in open-plan loft-style conversions. When introducing new structures, ensure they work with existing ones and select materials that complement any original textures. This contemporary dark, grained walnut unit beautifully enhances the tonal variations in the brick wall beyond.

OPPOSITE ABOVE CENTRE So much of our heritage lies in the fabric and structure of old industrial buildings. Centuries-old machinery and work tools are worth restoring and preserving for future generations. They also provide unique design features, such as this timber and rope pulley construction in a former maritime building in New York.

OPPOSITE ABOVE RIGHT Exposed brick is a favourite of urban pioneers. In its natural state, it can provide a warm, rich and tactile surface. For a cleaner look, apply a coat of paint. Here, white has been used to create a neutral backdrop against which a gallery of contrasting pictures and paintings can be displayed.

RIGHT Mezzanines will add visual impact to a high-ceilinged space and create additional floor space for a home office, spare bedroom or den. Use hardwearing materials such as steel, metal and wood to complement original structural elements. The most successful mezzanines are those that manage to retain a visual connection with the living space below.

Steel-framed windows, metal staircases and doors and pulley systems will add bags of style to the end result. When it comes to new materials, consider steel joists, wire-mesh glass and wide timber boards, all of which will add industrial flavour. For ex-commercial units, try ply flooring and steel-framed glass walls for a modern twist on utility chic. Even scaffolding poles can be repurposed into all sorts of domestic constructions, from sink units to shelf supports.

When factoring in plumbing and heating, source items that will add urban charm. Cast-iron radiators were originally designed for use in Victorian schools, factories and hospitals, and reclaimed originals can be sourced from salvage yards or specialist dealers. In the kitchen, exposed stainless steel ducting will add factory flair. Similarly, surface-mounted copper piping is a common attribute of municipal spaces and makes a great design feature in any industrial-inspired interior.

URBAN STYLE

ADD A DASH OF UTILITY CHIC with items designed and produced for the factories, warehouses and commercial buildings of the past. Devised to be functional and hardworking, such designs combine practicality with a sturdy, attractive aesthetic and nowadays are statement pieces highly sought after by urban pioneers wanting to add a dash of industrial style to their homes. Hunt down vintage originals or be inspired by contemporary alternatives and mix them with natural elements and reclaimed finds.

LIGHTING

Most iconic industrial lighting styles were created between the 1920s and 70s, and workplace lighting of this period marries form and function beautifully. Crafted from aluminium, steel, toughened glass, enamel and porcelain, classic factory pendants and task lamps make attractive additions to a domestic interior. Nautical lighting, such as passage and bulkhead lights,

was designed to be weatherproof and is thus ideal for areas like bathrooms. Strip lights are also enjoying a renaissance and can make a strong design statement in a kitchen, where good overhead lighting is essential.

Braided lighting flex/cable in black, white and brown will add an element of authenticity to any lighting scheme. Alternatively, opt for a brightly coloured modern version and loop the flex across the ceiling with the help of a hook ceiling rose. All sorts of fixtures, from bulb holders and suspension chains to switch plates and sockets, have had an old-fashioned makeover and are available in various metals as well as retro Bakelite and porcelain finishes. Edison-style filament bulbs ooze urban style and work well either as a bare bulb in a holder or combined with a metal cage shade.

Urban pioneers wanting to add industrial authenticity can source original pieces from salvage yards or vintage suppliers. Classics such as the Jieldé lamp, the Anglepoise, Lampe Gras and Bestlite ranges were designed to illuminate drafting tables and desks, so are architectural in design and well worth hunting down. Contemporary pendants in sleek copper or steel combine practicality with good design and look great against bare plaster or exposed brickwork.

OPPOSITE ABOVE LEFT Pared-down and superbly utilitarian in its design, a bedside light constructed from a bulb holder and protective cage shade casually hangs from a wire hook on a stand. Its simple aesthetic is perfectly in tune with the raw backdrop of the warehouse setting.

OPPOSITE ABOVE RIGHT Once used in factories, workshops and on drafting tables of the 1950s, the Jieldé light is a design classic. Here, a vintage model clearly showing signs of age with peeling paint and patches of rust elegantly illuminates the home owner's art collection.

ABOVE RIGHT The dimensions of some industrial pendant lights can be huge. Designed to be sizeable enough to illuminate vast workspaces, they are ideal for hanging in hallways and other large spaces. Here, a spun aluminium pendant brings some authentic charm to a former factory interior and is softened by a rustic-style chandelier decorated with foliage.

RIGHT Urban pioneering provides plenty of opportunity for repurposing ex-industrial components. This line of metal pendant shades hanging above the dining table in a London warehouse was constructed from discarded engine pistons. The rough patina of the metal is transformed to a luxurious sheen when lit up.

FURNITURE

Industry and the workplace have played a huge part in influencing many of the furniture designs that comprise the urban pioneer style. A number of contemporary chairs, tables, desks, storage units and beds are inspired by those once produced for factories, schools, hospitals, commercial units and even parks, and will add a functional, utilitarian vibe to a domestic setting. Original industrial designs tend to be robust, large and solid, built to withstand heavy daily usage on the factory floor. Favoured materials include solid wood, steel and galvanized metal and iron, with a basic range of muted industrial paint shades and powder-coated finishes available in later years. Many classic designs, such as the Tolix Model A chair or the Luxembourg stackable chair, have been reissued for today's market in bright colours that provide a bold and contemporary twist on a classic look.

It's well worth trying to source originals rather than reproductions if possible, as they are authentic and timeless in their appeal. Vintage height-adjustable machinist stools, classroom chairs, workbenches and

OPPOSITE Iconic Tolix chairs are instantly recognizable and add industrial flavour to a room. Designed by Xavier Pauchard in the 1930s and made from galvanized steel, they were originally designed as functional seating for factories, offices, hospitals and ships. In this converted garage, they are teamed with a suitably robust steel and wood dining table.

ABOVE LEFT Scaffolding poles and metal clamps are usually found on construction sites, but they can also be put to good use in a converted home. Here, they have been used to construct a chunky, robust frame for a dining table. The industrial metal casters allow the table to be easily moved if needed – handy in a large loft space.

ABOVE CENTRE Vintage machinist stools are widely available through specialist dealers and provide plenty of utilitarian style with their attractive time-worn patina. Comprising a metal base with a swivel mechanism, the height of the wooden seat is adjustable. These stools make great compact seating options as well as impromptu side tables.

ABOVE RIGHT Industrial catering equipment, both old and new, is practical and hardworking, and only looks better as it ages. Seek out vintage or second-hand pieces, such as metal trolleys, wire storage racks and stainless steel workbenches. There are also modern appliances such as cookers and extractor fans that enjoy retro industrial styling.

OPPOSITE ABOVE LEFT Classic designer pieces add an element of sophistication to a rough-hewn industrial interior. This iconic Arne Jacobsen bentwood chair creates a statement with its sublime combination of curvaceous form and practical function.

OPPOSITE ABOVE RIGHT Combine contrasting furniture styles to add interest to an urban conversion. A pair of elegant mid-century chairs is beautifully complemented by a factory cabinet and a coffee table made from reclaimed timber mounted on vintage trolley wheels.

OPPOSITE BELOW LEFT Take inspiration from the style of your industrial space. Factories of the Art Deco period often still retain the linear curves for which they are admired. Furniture from the same era and with similar detailing works wonderfully in such an interior.

OPPOSITE BELOW RIGHT Urban pioneers are adept at repurposing discarded objects. Here, old wooden ladders have been used to support wooden planks and together they form a quirky shelving unit and space divider.

RIGHT Mass-produced for use in textile factories, machinist chairs are height-adjustable with a curved backrest and slender cast-iron construction. They are robust but neat in style and make great modern-day kitchen bar stools.

even metal park benches are all favourites of the urban pioneer. Team them with dining tables constructed from reclaimed timber planks and steel structures that have been engineered with as much precision and force as an iron girder. The large scale of some pieces provides an opportunity to create interest within an industrial conversion where the room sizes and ceiling heights are similarly oversized. Large pieces can also be used to create a sense of drama in a smaller space.

Salvage yards, flea markets and junk shops are all good places to pick up items that can be repurposed.

Solid wood chests can be restyled into bathroom sink units, while utilitarian metal gym lockers and trunks are ideal storage solutions in any room.

Items that show signs of wear and tear are urban pioneer favourites. Chairs and sofas covered in worn fabric or battered leather and other pieces that are a bit shabby and ageing with rusty metal edging or scarred wood are all illustrative of a life well lived. In fact, any furniture piece that has a historical perspective will find it is well at home in these buildings that have enjoyed such an illustrious past.

DECORATIVE FINISHES

Creative decorative finishes can be used either to enhance the original fabric of former industrial buildings or to add much-needed interest and character to modern homes and newbuilds.

Practical and hardwearing, tiles have been used in commercial interiors for centuries. Originating in the brickmaking industry, terracotta floor tiles, with their warm red tones, sit well alongside stainless steel, exposed brick and wood, so are a great option for warehouse conversions. Patterned or encaustic tiles, meanwhile, will provide an unexpected decorative contrast to a gritty urban backdrop. Source batch ends from reclamation yards and specialist suppliers, and patchwork different tiles together for a unique look.

For classic utility chic in the bathroom or kitchen, you can't beat the basic white metro brick tile. As its name implies, it was widely used in train and metro stations as well as in prisons, hospitals and other public buildings. Classic white teamed with dark grey grouting will give maximum impact.

Tin tiles are high on the urban pioneer style agenda. Originally designed to provide an alternative to elaborate plaster ceilings, they were made from sheet metal pressed into moulds to create different patterns and then whitewashed to resemble aged plaster. When unpainted, their metallic finish means that they contrast beautifully with bare brick and concrete, and they can be used to cover an entire ceiling or hung on walls as an unusual decorative feature.

OPPOSITE LEFT Make wall art from salvaged pieces or personal mementos for a truly individual effect. Here, the owner's sizeable collection of licence plates has been wall mounted to form a colourful and graphic display.

OPPOSITE RIGHT Large-scale photographic prints, wallpapers and murals are ideal for adding detail to an otherwise featureless wall. For an urban-style interior, images of concrete, timber planks, metro bricks and tin tiles all work well, as this textural-looking headboard demonstrates.

BELOW Bold Moorish tiles add a bohemian flavour to this shower enclosure in an Art Deco factory conversion. Their geometric pattern and rich copper hue strike an exuberant decorative note in this tiny space.

Current decorative trends can also offer a shot of heritage charm. Look out for quirky wallpapers that are photographic representations of exposed brickwork, old filing drawers, concrete panels, tin tiles and timber planks. They are ideal for bringing some cheeky industrial chic to a modern space.

Wood panelling, such as tongue and groove, can also add interest to a bland interior. Its original purpose was to cover uneven surfaces, but it can be used decoratively as well as to provide an element of insulation. Paint is ideal for zoning areas, and is available in finishes that are sympathetic to old structures. Look out for breathable clay paints, and lime washes with an attractive chalky finish. Paints designed for industrial use, such as blackboard, enamel and metallic paints, are also ideal for kitchen cabinetry. Heavy-duty floor paints add colour to concrete and timber floors and are designed to be hardwearing. For an authentic industrial palette, opt for knocked-back shades such as Air Force blue, khaki and muddy taupe.

RIGHT The metro brick tile is hugely popular in industrial-inspired bathrooms. Here it has been strategically used as a practical decorative finish and to cleverly highlight a patch of structural brick that has been revealed under peeling plaster.

BELOW AND BOTTOM LEFT Packing blankets for wrapping furniture during removals have been repurposed as furnishing fabric and used to upholster this bed base and headboard. Made from recycled materials, the blankets are both utilitarian and eco-friendly. A pillow made from a coffee-bean sack and a military-inspired woollen throw completes the look.

FABRIC AND TEXTILES

Textiles are essential to the industrial urban home. Tactile fabrics and soft textures provide a sumptuous juxtaposition to concrete, metal and brick. And many fabrics, such as denim, hessian, linen, calico, ticking and wool, have been a huge part of industry over the centuries, so it makes sense that urban pioneers should choose them.

Cotton is a fabric staple, and its clean, crisp appearance makes it an ideal candidate for everyday bathroom, bedroom and kitchen textiles. Cotton ticking is a classic, with its distinctive stripe. Traditionally used to cover mattresses, nowadays ticking is a smart but functional choice for sofa and chair covers.

Linen is a more luxurious option and is revered for its slubby, uneven weave. Made from the fibres of the flax plant, it has been used throughout history by

BELOW RIGHT Large factory and warehouse spaces often require an element of partitioning between different areas to create smaller spaces and cosy corners suitable for different functions. Here, linen panels attached with simple metal pins to the wooden framework of a kitchen mezzanine provide a solution that is full of practicality and casual elegance. The loose weave of the linen also allows the sturdy structure of the raised platform to be revealed.

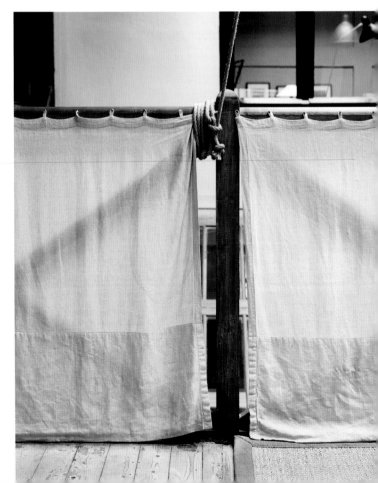

many industries due to its strength and durability. During World War II, the aircraft industry used unbleached linen to cover the control surfaces of aeroplanes. It was also widely used by fishermen for their nets and in hospitals for bedding, bandages and uniforms. Its relaxed, slightly crumpled appearance makes it ideal for bed linen, curtains and simple hanging dividers.

Heavy-duty denim, canvas and calico are usually associated with workplace uniforms, but their versatility and hardwearing credentials make them popular choices for urban interiors. Add some factory chic to a living space with a sofa cover or floor cushion in indigo denim or storage bags made from sturdy canvas.

Velvet, leather and sheepskin will all sit well against a tough industrial aesthetic and are perfect for adding an indulgent dash of luxury to an urban space. Wool, worsted, tweed, flannel and felt are all natural fibres and full of sensual warmth. Layer them on beds and sofas, or hang them as curtains to provide a soft contrast to raw brick walls. Look out for industrial blankets repurposed from recycled yarns and military versions sourced through army surplus outlets. With a heavy weight and virtually indestructible, such items were designed for maximum protection against the cold and wet, and are just right for the industrial interior.

ABOVE RIGHT Mixing different textiles and fabrics is the key to creating an urban home full of interest and warmth. Patterns, colours and textures can all be combined to achieve a style that is rich in visual and sensual appeal. This living area contains a generous sofa piled with scatter cushions and teamed with soft rugs for comfort underfoot.

RIGHT Dyed linen allows for rich jewel-like colours to be introduced into an interior scheme. Here, peacock blue and fuchsia pink pillows are teamed with a rich gold throw, bringing a note of decadence and luxury to this dark sleeping nook. The natural creases in the fabric are beautifully highlighted by the light falling from the tiny window.

ACCESSORIES

Many of the classic tools of industry are also the preferred accessories of the urban pioneer home. Designed and crafted to be tough and withstand heavy usage, many implements and objects that started life in former factories and workplaces are finding their way into our homes. All sorts of items, from canteen cookware and commercial pots and pans to factory clocks and machinists stools, can be sourced either via vintage stores and markets or by investing in new versions manufactured by many of the original companies that are still in existence.

Many items traditionally used in canteens and kitchens have gained iconic status. Well-engineered stainless steel toasters, kettles, mixers and weighing scales sit alongside simple white canteen serveware, enamel cookware, heavy-bottomed copper pans and classic glass preserving jars, as well as a range of utility goods such as brushes, brooms and galvanized dustpans, iron buckets and garbage cans.

Workplace items are also a firm favourite when it comes to transforming an urban home into one that oozes industrial chic. Restored steel filing cabinets, metal boxes and aluminium canisters, oversized factory and station clocks and wire baskets are all not only useful but also have a sturdy, no-nonsense aesthetic that makes them highly desirable objects. Even naval kit bags, market baskets and canvas holdalls can offer quirky storage options for any room.

Objects and implements designed for use in schools, hospitals and laboratories are great for adding a dash of industrial style to a bathroom. Enamel medical cabinets, specimen trays, apothecary jars, glass measuring beakers and other bits and pieces are all highly collectible and can easily be repurposed as soap dishes, toothbrush tumblers and storage containers.

OPPOSITE ABOVE LEFT Glass storage jars with rubber seals and metal clip fastenings are classic larder staples. Available in a range of sizes, they are ideal for storing a variety of dry foods.

OPPOSITE ABOVE CENTRE Rusty metal boxes may look like they have had their moment, but their time-aged patina is what makes them attractive.

OPPOSITE ABOVE RIGHT Industrial in scale and strength, commercial cooking implements made from robust stainless steel are ideal utilitarian kitchen accessories. Canteen-style straining spoons, ladles and sieves are all built to last.

OPPOSITE BELOW LEFT Tools can double up as ornaments. This nicely curated collection of tailor's scissors and sewing accessories means they are also close to hand when needed.

OPPOSITE BELOW CENTRE Once a canteen favourite, the classic Duralex tumbler is right at home in an urban context. Tough and stackable, it is a perfect example of functional design at its best.

OPPOSITE BELOW RIGHT The best pots and pans are made from industrial-strength materials such as copper, stainless steel and heat-resistant enamel. Source them from commercial kitchen suppliers to ensure top-quality and long-lasting performance.

ABOVE Even the most functional of items can form part of a display. This assembled selection of objects on a sideboard includes large glass apothecary jars filled with pearl light bulbs and a set of Fornasetti dinner plates hung on the wall. Collectively, they create an eye-catching display.

THIS PAGE The lofty scale of warehouse interiors offers plenty of space for oversized, jungly houseplants. Here, they add visual interest to an otherwise redundant corner. A simple zinc container offsets the rich glossy green of the leaves perfectly and provides sufficient room for further growth. Plants of different shapes and sizes are essential ingredients in an urban home, creating a powerful connection with the natural world.

NATURAL ELEMENTS

Adding splashes of greenery and rustic textures to an urban interior will provide welcome respite from unyielding concrete and metal surfaces. Inner-city warehouses and other buildings are often devoid of any outdoor space, so creating a small urban jungle in a corner of a room is the perfect way of bringing a little bit of the outside in.

Plants make great additions to the home for lots of reasons. They absorb carbon dioxide and enhance air quality in the process. They also look good, and with so many different leaf, stem and flower formations, they contribute visual interest in an instant. Potted plants are easy to maintain and create attractive displays when grouped together. Try lacy ferns, sculptural cacti, scented geraniums or tiny succulents. Galvanized metal buckets and canisters, concrete pots, recycled rubber tyre planters and repurposed steel ducting all make quirky and upbeat containers. Alternatively, an elegant terrarium is a great way of displaying smaller plants in an indoor botanical garden.

Flowers are ideal for adding a dash of colour and life. Flower markets are the best source of unusual foliage, pods and other forms of vegetation that will visually enliven a room and fill it with natural fragrance.

Introduce objects fashioned from natural fibres for some homespun charm. Willow, rush and wicker baskets bring organic texture and form to any room. Source shapes and styles that have a warmth and personality about them and that are handwoven and well made. Anything that combines practicality with a simple decorative aesthetic will fit perfectly.

ABOVE The natural texture and tones of a pair of woven willow log baskets and the chopped logs that they contain provide a visual respite from the vast white expanse of the interior.

ABOVE A glass and metal terrarium is ideal for container gardening. Perched on a vintage potting table with space underneath for tools, pots and string, it makes an attractive indoor nature display.

ABOVE Elements of nature can be hugely practical: here, a pretty woven basket provides the owner with storage for fruit. Baskets are practical, beautiful to look at and tactile.

REAL URBAN SPACES

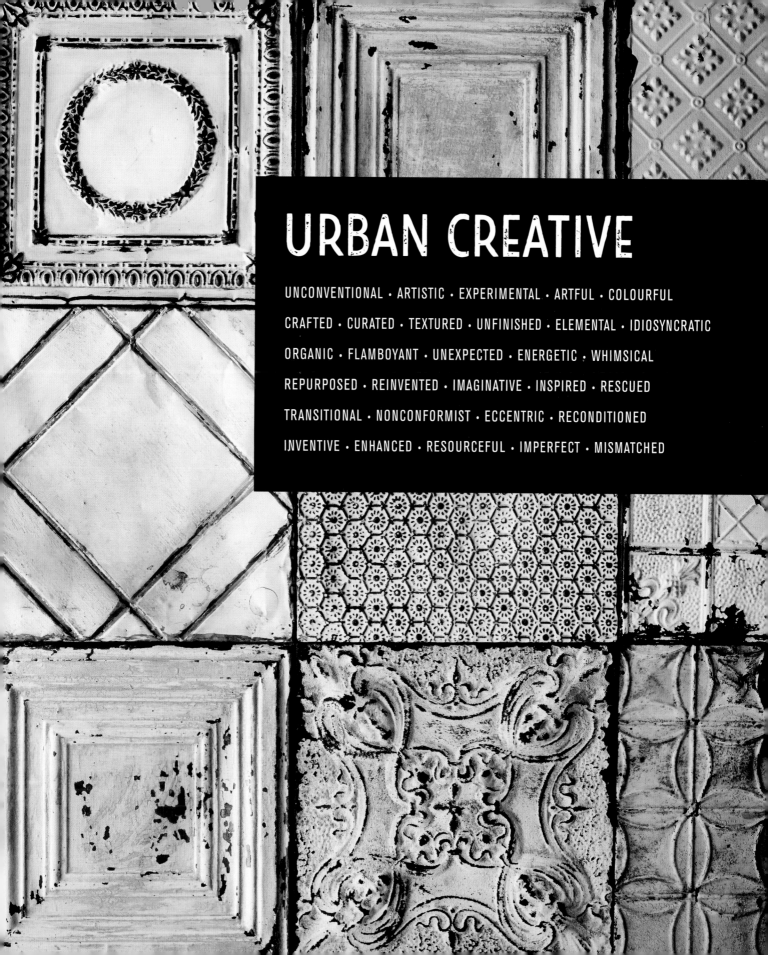

URBAN CREATIVE

UNCONVENTIONAL · ARTISTIC · EXPERIMENTAL · ARTFUL · COLOURFUL
CRAFTED · CURATED · TEXTURED · UNFINISHED · ELEMENTAL · IDIOSYNCRATIC
ORGANIC · FLAMBOYANT · UNEXPECTED · ENERGETIC · WHIMSICAL
REPURPOSED · REINVENTED · IMAGINATIVE · INSPIRED · RESCUED
TRANSITIONAL · NONCONFORMIST · ECCENTRIC · RECONDITIONED
INVENTIVE · ENHANCED · RESOURCEFUL · IMPERFECT · MISMATCHED

OPPOSITE AND RIGHT Create warmth and intimacy in an open-plan loft with a dark palette and a sophisticated mix of industrial-style and vintage furniture and accessories. In the dining area, an intense blue shade on the walls complements the rich browns of the bare brick and the wooden cabinet and dining table. The leather chairs add a sleeker note, while the rust on the pendant lights, made from reconditioned engine pistons, highlights the tones in the brick beautifully. Industrial-style accessories, including a factory clock and a New York City Subway sign, complete the look.

BELOW A pocket of outside space has been transformed into a tiny courtyard garden. Accessed via a door off the kitchen, it provides Peter with views over the city rooftops and just enough space for alfresco dining. Metal chain curtains hang at the doors. Their robust design will add some industrial style to a window or doorway.

EAST MEETS EAST

A FORMER CARPENTER'S WAREHOUSE in the heart of London's hip Shoreditch has been transformed into a space that is beautifully flamboyant in its dark sophistication, despite the backdrop of unfinished brick and industrial wood. Its owner's ambition was to transform a somewhat unconventional shell into a warm and welcoming home with a bold, idiosyncratic aesthetic.

Dating back to the late 1800s, this building is an architectural remnant of what was once the East End of London's thriving furniture district, where designers, craftsmen, manufacturers and showrooms existed side by side in an industrial hub that lasted well into the 20th century. However, advancements in

manufacturing and competition from elsewhere led to its decline and the warehouses slowly became vacant. The area entered a long decline until the *enfants terrible* of London's contemporary art scene – Damien Hirst, Gary Hume, Tracey Emin et al – were attracted to these cheap, capacious spaces as ideal places in which to create and exhibit their work. Other creative industries and cultural outlets soon followed suit and the area thrived. Before long, old warehouses and redundant factories were in demand as cool urban alternatives to more conventional residential spaces.

For owner Peter, returning from living and working in Bangkok for several years, the

LEFT Classic industrial materials and design ideas are in abundance in Peter's kitchen. Aluminium chequer plate sheeting, used as an anti-slip surface in commercial workspaces, has been re-employed here as a kitchen plinth and splashback. Steel ducting was left exposed and a salvaged vintage work trolley has been given a new life as storage for cookery books.

OPPOSITE Peter has repeated the pillar-box red used on the kitchen shelf and breakfast bar on the door that leads to the dining room from the hallway, while the door handle is the same as those used on the kitchen cabinets. Repeating motifs in this way can create a link between two large spaces, in this case the kitchen and dining areas.

RIGHT A wealth of natural elements makes the living space a warm and welcoming part of the loft. Located in the centre of the space, the two generously sized sofas have been upholstered in a richly coloured kelim fabric and are strategically positioned at right angles to create a cosy spot centred on the fireplace. Chunky reclaimed wood and rustic textures provide elements of the natural world, and the leaf shapes of the faux plants throw stunning shadow effects when the lamps and fire are lit.

LEFT Peter has piled the sofas with soft sheepskin cushions and tactile animal hides to add comfort to his eclectic living space.

area's buzzing creative energy was a huge attraction. The neighbourhood – central and close to his place of work – was in the throes of development and the brick facades of the old warehouses were a refreshing contrast to the glass and steel towers starting to mushroom in the financial district nearby.

Keen to make his loft workable yet sociable, Peter sectioned off part of the large open-plan living and dining area to make a quiet, secluded home office tucked away from the main space. A custom-built shelving-unit-cum-room-divider cleverly separates the interior and provides storage space on both sides. The rest of the main area is configured into discrete zones for different activities. The kitchen

FAR LEFT Photographic wallpaper is ideal for adding a creative touch to an otherwise plain wall. Look out for designs by celebrated designer Deborah Bowness that depict various scenarios such as piled deed boxes, utility chairs and, as shown here, the 'Genuine Fake Books' design. Peter has used it as a playful backdrop for a console table and pair of old trunks.

and dining areas are semi-screened by a breakfast bar that has a handy raised panel so that the oven/stove, sink and worksurfaces are hidden from view.

The original chimneybreast and fireplace create a dramatic focal point, and Peter has tucked the sofa and chairs towards it to create a cosy seating arrangement, particularly in winter when the fire is in use. The piano, on the other hand, has been placed in the far corner, where light streams in through the double windows. In addition, Peter has created pockets of interest throughout the space that provide an injection of personality. Photographic wallpapers – bookshelves in

ABOVE LEFT Quirky and creative, Peter's loft is full of elements of surprise. A standard lamp and a plaid curtain provide a dash of English eccentricity and are practical too. The thick curtains insulate the loft from draughts during the colder months, and the lamp creates atmosphere with its soft pool of light.

LEFT Large open-plan spaces benefit from inventive ways to separate and enclose individual areas. In Peter's home, a custom-built bookcase-cum-room divider sections off the home office from the main living space. A gap at the top of the unit allows the overall interior to retain a sense of connection.

ABOVE Create interesting scenarios within a large open space with innovative furniture groupings. Peter's piano and chair have been given a central position in the living area and benefit from light flooding in from the nearby window.

OPPOSITE Position furniture strategically to balance uneven architectural features. Here, the slightly disparate proportions of a window and an adjoining door are played down thanks to the placing of a large, prominent wooden cabinet, while the accompanying low table adds to the asymmetrical effect and keeps things interesting.

the living room and tin tiles on the sides of the breakfast bar and used as a headboard in the bedroom – are visual quirks that provide a welcome respite from the natural brick. Similarly, Peter has added plenty of decorative anachronisms that depart from the classic industrial aesthetic, such as a standard lamp with an old-fashioned lampshade, a full-length plaid curtain and a whimsical menagerie of pottery birds and animals.

Added to this eclectic mix are some sturdy pieces of furniture that Peter bought back from Bangkok, such as the custom-built kitchen storage cabinet, the tailor-

made sofa and the solid Arts and Crafts-style wooden bed, which, all things considered, seem quite fitting bearing in mind both the owner's Eastern connections and the original role of this East London warehouse.

One of the most successful elements in this interior is Peter's use of a rich dark blue on the walls. These were previously white and Peter started off painting one feature wall in the inky blue shade. He was so smitten that he went on to apply it to the entire living space and then the ceiling too. The intense blue hue elevates the original brickwork from its utilitarian

LEFT Peter has created a retro 1970s-style home office with walnut veneer cupboards and a collection of chunky accessories in muted shades of burnt orange and turquoise. The subtle shades enhance the natural tones in the brickwork as well as adding to the intimate mood of the apartment. A low table and lamp and an animal hide rug contribute warmth and create a connection with the main living space.

OPPOSITE LEFT The compact bedroom is full of industrial references and clever takes on heritage style. Tin tile wallpaper acts as a statement headboard, and the solidly constructed wooden bed with its pared-down linen bedcover is the embodiment of utilitarian simplicity. Only a fur throw hints at luxury.

ABOVE Peter has added his own sense of style to the bathroom. Ubiquitous white metro tiles, grey grouting and stainless steel fixtures have been given a warm and contemporary twist with clean-lined walnut storage cupboards similar to those in the home office. The walls are a deep charcoal shade that serves to connect the space with the rest of the apartment.

origins and transforms it into a rich, sophisticated finish. The large warehouse windows create pools of light at each end of the space, while the dark, tonal colour palette casts deep shadows. In the evenings, Peter turns on an assortment of lamps dotted around the apartment to create a cosy and intimate mood.

As Peter travels a great deal, he has filled his home with an assortment of lush greenery that is, he admits, fashionably faux. Regularly topped up with vases of fresh flowers from nearby Columbia Road Flower Market, the leafy ferns and palms and small bowls of cacti and succulents add vibrant green hues to the decor. They also create a visual link with a tiny roof terrace – a highly valued pocket of outside space tucked in among the city's rooftops that Peter has crammed with plenty of nature's best.

FAR LEFT Successful design marries beauty and performance, and many everyday objects are also revered for their display credentials, as the shapely components of this 1950s coffee service and vintage signage demonstrate.

LEFT Originally used for drying glass as well as wrapping bread, meat and fish, the humble linen glass cloth can add a dash of utility chic to any kitchen. Source traditional versions with a jaunty red or blue stripe.

BELOW AND OPPOSITE An expansive open-plan loft in its original post-industrial state is something of a holy grail for urban pioneers and provides the perfect backdrop for a creative mix of interior styles. Here, a polished concrete floor and chunky original pipes form a robust framework for a mix of styles, from cupboard doors made out of reclaimed wood (below) to sleek designer chairs and elegant decorative lighting (opposite).

PERFECTLY IMPERFECT

STANDING IN THIS WATERSIDE WAREHOUSE in Brooklyn, New York is to exist in a rare moment in time where the past and future seem to be as one. Outside, urban decay has taken hold of abandoned ex-industrial buildings where windows are broken, walls are covered with graffiti and nature untamed. The outlook for this entire area may seem bleak, but it is in fact very bright indeed.

This building is just one of 16 that were originally part of the vast Bush Terminal, a manufacturing, warehousing and shipping complex built on the Brooklyn waterfront towards the end of the 19th century. With an illustrious past and boasting to be the first facility of this type in New York, the terminal enjoyed many years of expansion until the Great Depression, when it fell into a steep decline. It wasn't until

the 1980s that the area embarked upon a massive process of reinvention and a restoration programme was implemented to preserve these historic warehouses for the future. Nowadays, the neighbourhood is known as Industry City and is once again flourishing as a base for creative industries and small businesses.

Stylist Carin Scheve and her family were drawn to the area by the affordable rents. Their live/workspace is situated on the outskirts of Industry City and boasts a heady mix of original features and industrial grit teamed with a huge 650 square metres/7000 square feet of floor space. For Carin and her husband Francesco, the initial attraction was the open-plan layout, the vast dimensions and the pared-down post-industrial aesthetic. The building's original steel-framed windows wrap around two sides of the loft and provide panoramic views over the Hudson River to the Statue of Liberty and the highrises of Lower Manhattan beyond, and while some panes are cracked and a little draughty, it seems a small price to pay for such spectacular original features and a view that could be considered priceless.

Throughout the interior, stout concrete columns, oversized heating elements, exposed pipework and poured concrete floors combine to create a living space that remains true to its past. As the area becomes gentrified, Carin and Francesco wonder how many spaces like this will

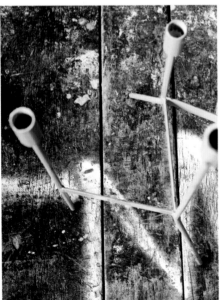

ABOVE Small pops of colour can unify a light, white space comprised of various different elements and styles. The utilitarian red stripe of an army surplus blanket acts as a visual reference, highlighting other splashes of red such as the painted pipework on the ceiling and the kitchen accessories seen behind.

LEFT AND OPPOSITE ABOVE
Repurposing old objects and materials means embracing signs of wear and tear to find an intrinsic beauty in something that would otherwise be discarded as past its sell-by date. Paint-spattered timber boards, a rusty metal frame and some salvaged trolley casters now enjoy a new life as a much-loved coffee table.

survive, as redevelopments so often remove the character and soul of an old building. The secret with post-industrial renovations is to know when to leave something alone and the couple have managed just that, adding only a couple of walls in order to section off an office space and fitting wire-mesh gates to create a prop storage area. They installed kitchen cabinets and updated some of the plumbing and electrical wiring, but that aside the space is as close to its original state as it can be.

RIGHT Carin's prop storage area doubles as a visual display in the cavernous open-plan interior. The couple sourced the wire-mesh doors that section off the area from a salvage yard. The props corner is an Aladdin's cave of furniture and accessories that remains on view through the metal doors while still removed from the main loft space.

THIS PAGE The loft retains many distinguishing features that are original to the space. While not always as efficient as their modern equivalents, the metal-framed windows, ceiling-mounted piping and oversized tubular radiators are powerful reminders of our industrial heritage and are well worth retaining.

ABOVE LEFT TO RIGHT An armchair has been stripped back to its wooden frame, revealing a grid of rusty coil springs, jute tension webbing and neat lengths of twine. The result is an object of pared-back beauty. Made from pure sheep's wool, the Swiss Army blanket is a military staple that dates back to the end of the 19th century and provides utilitarian style with timeless appeal. Sturdy cotton calico is used as a lining in traditional upholstery. A soft oatmeal colour, it possesses plenty of visual appeal when exposed.

FAR RIGHT Carin's deconstructed sofa and armchairs are in keeping with the unadorned industrial aesthetic of the loft. From the back, the sofa offers intriguing detailing. The fitted cover and padding have been removed to reveal the raw wooden frame and jute webbing beneath.

For Carin, the raw, deconstructed aesthetic of her home is part of the intrinsic appeal of warehouse living and it's something that she embraces wholeheartedly. As a stylist, she is constantly seeking beauty in the everyday, whether in the form of a frayed remnant of patterned silk or the rich patina of a battered old leather armchair. Her 'finding beauty in imperfection' philosophy is apparent throughout her home, from the simple timber and metal bed to the armchairs and sofa, which have been stripped back to the framework and springs with just their calico lining remaining and are dressed with utilitarian army surplus blankets and sheepskins.

The loft is a constantly evolving space. Carin likes to change and transform the interior at whim as part of an ongoing experiment in reinvention and reuse. Vintage stepladders and timber planks

OPPOSITE A poured concrete floor is low maintenance and hardwearing. It can be polished to a high sheen or coloured using a specially formulated primer and paint. Carin has painted a darker grey square to zone off the area of floor space that contains the bed.

FAR LEFT Industrial lighting options are never overly flamboyant or ostentatious in design. A metal cage light made of steel and wood is simple in form but elegant in its wiry skeletal structure.

LEFT A rough wood and steel frame has been repurposed into an urban pioneering alternative to a conventional bed.

BELOW A shapely vintage chair adds pared-down sophistication to the bedroom area. Its woven webbing echoes the exposed framework of the sofa and armchairs.

have been cleverly repurposed as makeshift shelving and also act as informal space dividers, while an oversized ornate glass chandelier is suspended from a tubular metal strut. Every now and then Carin will raid the props cage and introduce elements that refresh and update the interior. Whatever takes her fancy gets thrown into the mix, yet somehow everything hangs together perfectly thanks to Carin's many years of experience as a prop stylist.

This is a sociable space, and the large kitchen/dining area has been designed expressly for entertaining and get-togethers. The couple rent the loft out for photographic shoots and events or to clients wanting a space to host projects in, and often Francesco will bring his Vespa scooter in to work on it.

LEFT AND ABOVE Turning a pair of old stepladders into shelving is a simple and effective storage solution. Carin has arranged two ladders with several timber planks in between to provide display space and storage for books and objects. The ladders' 'A' frames counteract the many horizontals in the loft, and the shelving unit doubles up as a section divider within the open-plan interior.

BELOW AND OPPOSITE In the bathroom area, classic loft style meets minimal Japanese Zen. Furniture and accessories here have been chosen for their serene simplicity and modest design, which fuses beauty with practicality. Decorative twig sculptures sit alongside equally striking woven pieces such as this shallow basket that holds bath towels.

As a result, nothing is fixed here and when necessary the main space can quickly be cleared or the loft's contents swapped around.

Carin and Francesco's loft is the true embodiment of urban pioneering and post-industrial reinvention. As well as being a much-loved home, the warehouse is once again functioning as a busy workspace and in this way it mirrors the rejuvenation of the surrounding area. Hopefully Industry City can follow the lead of this pioneering couple and successfully retain elements of its former life as it embraces what promises to be a dazzling future ahead.

FAR LEFT Amsterdam's floating flower market on the Singel Canal has been providing locals with flora since 1862. Jennifer prefers a mix of individual stems and displays them in coloured vases to complement the bright hues of the tapestry wall art.

LEFT Two vintage artillery canisters have been turned into makeshift planters. Their galvanized surface and stencilled typography add a charming urban contrast to the tranquil Buddha head.

BELOW The soaring height of the walls offers the couple plenty of space to display artworks. One wall is filled entirely with Jennifer's enormous grid of vintage needlepoint, consisting of more than 100 pieces that she has collected over the years. Each individual canvas has been separately stretched and mounted and then all of them have been joined together in one large installation.

COOL CANTEEN

THE IMPACT ON THE URBAN ENVIRONMENT of history's economic booms is evident in the vast proportions of the industrial units constructed during those times. Enormous factories and warehouses dominated certain parts of towns and cities, and paternalistic employers wishing to improve the quality of life of their workers also constructed social spaces built on a similar scale.

This long, low concrete building in Amsterdam's eastern docklands is one such construction. It was built in the early 1900s as a canteen for dockworkers at the KNSM (Royal Dutch Steamboat Shipping Company) headquarters and docks in Amsterdam. Built on stilts with long windows overlooking the water, the canteen was originally accessed via a monumental staircase at one end of the building.

THIS PAGE The high ceilings of the canteen allowed for the construction of a mezzanine level that provides space for two bedrooms and a bathroom, which enjoy panoramic views over the water as well as an abundance of natural light.

THIS PAGE The couple have used bold tones to delineate different spaces. For example, the kitchen's rich, leafy green hue differentiates the cooking zone from the blue dining area. On the walls are a large framed wallhanging of a windmill made from old socks and picked up in a street market in Estonia and an abstract painting by Jennifer.

THIS PAGE AND OPPOSITE ABOVE The lounge area is below the mezzanine level, so has an intimate, den-like feel. Plenty of urban elements, including a distressed leather lounge chair, boxy sofa, 1970s-style pendant shade and a coffee table created from a vintage Swiss rifle pallet, provide a laid-back retro vibe.

Impressive in size and with an open-plan configuration, the canteen was filled with long tables and enough chairs to accommodate up to 1500 workers for meals and breaks throughout the day. It also doubled as a central community space for twice-yearly events that brought all the KNSM employees together.

The area fell into dereliction when the steamship industry itself went into decline and moved from the island to another location. Like so many abandoned industrial buildings, the empty canteen caught the attention of a group of young artists who took advantage of Holland's famously lax attitude towards squatting and moved in. By the 1990s, the entire area embarked upon a programme of regeneration and transformation into a residential area. However,

as there was only one staircase in the building that was a viable fire escape, the canteen did not meet the local housing corporation's criteria for conversion, and the squatters were offered it at a token price. By sheer coincidence, the building's inhabitants subsequently stumbled upon six old ship staircases that they fitted as 'flying' staircases, enabling the transformation of the building into eight loft spaces, each with its own access and exit.

Today, the building is a creative hub of work/live units that attracts designers, artists and architects. For Jennifer and her

LEFT Jennifer's collection of family licence plates dating back to the Great Depression hangs on the wall like a family quilt. The montage, inspired by work seen in Amsterdam's Stedelijk Museum, creates an immediate feeling of truly being at home surrounded by family history and is Jennifer's most treasured personal possession.

THIS PAGE Jennifer and Liam have amassed so many collectibles over the years that the canteen's vast proportions act rather like a gallery space. From Haitian barber signs, military gas masks and vintage tailor's dummies to skateboards and old sunglasses, the couple are adept at presenting their collections in dramatic and cohesive ways. The library bookshelves are stuffed with art and fashion books and work files, and are actually made from stacked picnic tables.

TINA MODOTTI
LE MANI DEL BURATTINAIO 1929

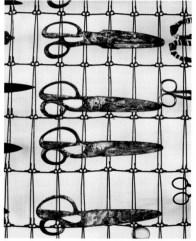

FAR LEFT An assortment of vintage and modern machinist tools and accessories is on display on the sewing station. This is positioned at the rear of the apartment, which is dedicated to the more practical aspects of the couple's daily lives. The arrangement is in a constant state of flux as the couple find more pieces to add to their burgeoning collections.

LEFT AND BELOW Liam is a fashion designer and tailor, and his scissor collection, amassed from around the world, is a prized possession that symbolizes his creative passions. Mounted on a vintage metal bedframe, the scissors make a unique industrial-inspired personal display.

husband Liam, the building's history and its former use as a place for congregating and socializing was as much of an attraction as the versatile living space their apartment provides. The apartment is both their home and their workplace, as it doubles up as a studio for their fashion business, and Jennifer and Liam wanted to incorporate all elements of their daily lives within the space while also zoning it according to task and function. As a result, the decor is hardworking and utilitarian at the 'work' end, and more decorative and sophisticated at the other.

The couple have made confident decorative choices, including rich paint colours, the thoughtful positioning of furniture and numerous displays of personal mementos dotted throughout the interior. Arrays of vintage scissors collected by Liam vie for attention with a handmade tapestry on one wall and Jennifer's collection of licence plates on another.

LEFT The work area is constantly in use for the couple's assorted creative endeavours, which range from devising the styling for a fashion show to a photo shoot to editing a video. All such activities can take place within this highly versatile space, once the garment rails (repurposed from a vintage set of gymnastic bars) have been pushed out of the way and additional chairs lifted down from the storage hooks above.

OPPOSITE The bespoke 'wallpaper' that covers the wall in the main bedroom is actually created from illustrations cut out of an oversized coffee-table book. The pages were removed by Jennifer and attached to the wall with the help of a tall ladder and a large tub of wallpaper paste.

Clothing rails hold collections in the making and spare chairs hooked up out of the way resemble an art installation. Even the spaces with specific roles, such as the garment archive, sewing station and tool storage area, are visual feasts as well as being highly practical.

The couple removed various elements that the squatters had introduced but they retained some of the original features, like the steelwork skeleton construction created by a local metal artist. Exposed trusses and concrete structures original to the building have been left on show, while the original canteen sink has been repurposed as a filing cabinet. A new concrete and resin floor has been laid throughout to unify the space and to create a rugged surface. A generously sized open-plan kitchen-cum-dining space was added to the river side of the apartment, making full use of the remarkable views over the water. It is constantly utilized by the couple as a social space for entertaining friends and clients, which seems entirely fitting considering the building's former purpose.

OPPOSITE AND RIGHT The kitchen has been given a blast of colour with strips of printed packing tapes applied to the original kitchen cabinets in a geometric pattern. The final result resembles a graphic contemporary artwork and has great impact in this small space. The juxtaposition of various different pendant lights creates a statement above the breakfast bar.

BELOW Houssein's interior style is an eccentric mix of the old and the new. The tiny kitchen packs a punch with Warhol's iconic screen print of Marilyn Monroe positioned alongside a rusty American dairy industry sign. Vintage advertising signage with striking typographical designs can be sourced from reclamation yards or online specialists.

VINTAGE MODERN

APPLYING A ROBUST, FACTORY-INSPIRED AESTHETIC to a compact modern interior may not be an obvious design choice. However, this quirky apartment in the heart of Manhattan possesses plenty of personality despite its tiny proportions and is the perfect example of how a creative eye and a cache of vintage finds can bring urban pioneer chic to even the most modest of spaces.

Situated in the fashionable neighbourhood of Chelsea, what this pocket-sized pad (just 87 square metres/936 square feet) lacks in size, it makes up for in terms of location: on the doorstep are New York's vibrant art galleries and hip bars and restaurants. It's part of a modern block and allows owner

Houssein Jarouche to enjoy a downtown lifestyle at a fraction of the cost of the large industrial loft conversions for which the area is famous. The rather undistinguished modern building is a practical compromise but it's one that works perfectly, bearing in mind that the apartment is only home to the native Brazilian during the four trips to New York he makes each year.

Houssein runs creative retail outlet and design business MiCASA in his home town of São Paulo, specializing in interior design, art and American collectibles. He visits New York regularly to source items at the city's flea markets and thrift stores. Many of his purchases are stored in the apartment before being crated up and shipped to Brazil. For Houssein, buying is not just his job but his passion, and his bijou New York base is testament to his creative vision and nonconformist attitude to interior design.

ABOVE A dark charcoal grey works well as a backdrop to industrial details and is both practical and dramatic. Here it sets the scene for Houssein's array of classic American collectibles, as well as drawing the eye into the bright main living space. The hallway cupboards have been painted the same colour and blend into the walls.

RIGHT AND OPPOSITE Every inch of this compact interior bears witness to the owner's magpie-like tendencies. The shelving unit and its contents are an essay in display, where a cornucopia of varied industrial and workplace items comes together as a visual record of his passion for vintage pieces.

When Houssein purchased the apartment, it was
very basic and felt significantly smaller. Eager to add
some personality and charm, he enlisted the help of
friend and New York interior designer Ana Strumpf,
and together the duo have created a look that is
colourful, creative and upbeat. A moody shade of
charcoal in the entrance hall and the kitchen visually
sections off the functional parts of the apartment and
draws the eye to an open-plan living and sleeping space
that is white, bright and flooded with light, thanks
to the 3.5-metre-/11-feet-high windows. The intense,
nearly black shade also serves as a scene setter for the
industrial pieces scattered throughout the apartment.
There are various salvaged ex-factory items, including
a metal-framed dining table that has been teamed with
an eclectic mix of mismatched vintage chairs to provide

OPPOSITE ABOVE
Tin tiles are an authentic feature of many American factories, workplaces and domestic interiors, created as an affordable decorative alternative to elaborate plaster ceiling mouldings. Originals can be sourced at flea markets and either used individually as wall art or on the ceiling, as intended. The ceiling is first covered with plywood and then the tin tiles are nailed in place. For a truly authentic feel, paint them off-white and sand lightly to reveal the raised detailing.

OPPOSITE BELOW LEFT AND RIGHT
Houssein's sturdy industrial-style shelving is home to vintage suitcases, industrial metal canisters and perforated steel baskets, all of which double as storage containers.

a relaxed sense of style. The same idea has been applied to the kitchen lighting, with different glass pendant lights, metal shades and bare bulbs hanging on random lengths of fabric flex/cable above the dining table.

Houssein is adept at tracking down objects that he loves and combining them successfully. He has adopted many display techniques used by galleries and museums, creating curated collections throughout his apartment. The walls are covered with an assortment of Houssein's treasured Pop Art canvases, contemporary artworks and quirky exhibits. A group of taxidermied impala heads hangs above the bed and a large vintage metal industrial sign dominates the wall opposite. The pièce de résistance, however, has to be the patchwork of original tin tiles on the ceiling. Houssein painstakingly sourced them one by one to recreate an authentically American design element.

The apartment is full of clever design ideas, all of which are simple enough to translate to any interior. The original kitchen cabinets have been given a

makeover with strips of brightly coloured duct tape that create a busy geometric pattern. The bed is covered in utilitarian transit blankets that are generally used to protect furniture during house removals. Similarly, an old coffee-bean sack has been repurposed as a pillow and sits alongside a medical-style blanket.

Houssein has amassed a vast treasure trove of salvaged, found, reconditioned and recycled pieces that he displays on a 4-metre/13-feet shelving unit that spans the whole length of the living space. Everything from rusty metal boxes and vintage light bulbs to original packaging and metal signage is on show here

This apartment is an Aladdin's cave of curios and personal mementos, one that is constantly reinvented and updated with new pieces that find their way back from the local flea markets and into Houssein's eclectic industrial-inspired interior.

ABOVE AND TOP
A vintage trunk creates a handy bedside table and offers invaluable storage space too. The soft green patina is echoed in the recycled glass vase and stems of silvery eucalyptus. The charming bedside lamp has been fashioned from a utilitarian metal stand with a double bulb holder and a whimsical decorative bird. Houssein has chosen filament bulbs for a vintage effect.

THIS PAGE AND
OPPOSITE LEFT
Grouping items of a similar
style is an effective display
idea that works well in small
spaces. Houssein has used
this device in many places
to add personality and style.
The impala heads arranged
on the wall, the various
pendant shades hanging in a
row and even the bed pillows
with different typographic
detailing are all prominent
collections that catch the eye
within the open-plan space.

URBAN BOHO

ECLECTIC · EMBELLISHED · DECORATIVE · RELAXED · TEXTURED · NATURAL

FADED · CAREFREE · LAYERED · PATINATED · WEATHERED · TARNISHED

SOPHISTICATED · AVANT-GARDE · ADORNED · RUSTIC · LUXURIOUS · RICH

JEWELLED · RETRO · SENSUAL · VINTAGE · INDULGENT · FANCIFUL · SLEEK

GLEAMING · MODERN · POLISHED · LUSTROUS · PATTERNED · MISMATCHED

ANTIQUE · EMBROIDERED · DECADENT

BELOW Louise's theatrical background has influenced her interior design choices. A juxtaposition of similar items in different styles provides a clever link between the entrance hall and main living space. On one side of the opening is a monochrome arrangement of a theatrical plaster bust on a plinth set against a dark background, while on the other a pastel-hued 1930s figurine sits on a modern sideboard in front of a white wall. The combination sets the scene for the bohemian and eclectic interior beyond.

DECO DELIGHT

THIS CONVERTED FACTORY BUILDING IN London's East End superbly illustrates industrial design at its best. A 1930s Art Deco building originally used to manufacture aircraft parts, it now houses a creative community that is drawn to its live/work lofts due to their unique aesthetic, which fuses the grittiness of industrial design with the exuberant architectural detailing for which the Art Deco style is renowned.

Designed by Sir Owen Williams, one of the leading architects of the time, the de Havilland building is an outstanding example of Art Deco architecture. The facade – all sweeping curves, dynamic horizontals and huge metal-framed windows – exemplifies the confident face

THIS PAGE AND OPPOSITE ABOVE The living
room is a magical mix of colours, textures and objects. Classic
Art Deco pieces sit alongside oriental accessories and a palette
of earthy terracotta and saffron yellow. Despite expectations
that she would paint the beamed concrete ceiling white, Louise
retained its raw finish but softened the effect with the subtle
hues of the decorative pieces.

ABOVE A reclaimed Belfast/farmhouse sink has been installed in the kitchen. Made from stain-resistant ceramic and generous in their proportions, these robust, utilitarian sinks are hugely practical and have an unpretentious, homely feel.

that architecture and industrial design adopted during the social and economic turmoil of the 1930s. Testament to the building's successful conversion to loft-style housing is the fact that units here are highly sought after by those seeking an inspiring place to call home.

With a floor space of approximately 111 square metres/1200 square feet and an interior that was no more than an empty shell with basic electrical and plumbing connections, owner Louise Miller was instantly attracted to the undeveloped loft space. She liked the building's history as well as the surrounding area, not least because this building and others nearby have attracted a spectrum of creative folk to the neighbourhood.

THIS PAGE The kitchen has a bright and breezy feel with plenty of boho charm. The encaustic tiles add pattern and colour, and create a wraparound effect that unites the dining area and kitchen as one zone. The tiling also cleverly forms a mid-height visual marker, effectively 'lowering' the ceiling.

OPPOSITE The wall between the kitchen and bathroom encompasses several reclaimed windows and pieces of coloured glass that act like a stained-glass window, casting varying shades of light into the living area to create a warm, intimate mood. The feature results in a rich, almost jewelled effect that is a direct contrast to the rough concrete ceiling. Louise has also incorporated small alcoves into the wall to provide storage for glassware and china. The refectory bench is the ideal length for Louise's custom-built scaffolding dining table and, together with the church chairs, adds a slight ecclesiastical flavour.

RIGHT A vintage metal cot/crib has been repurposed as a container for an indoor jungle that boasts an assortment of exotic leafy specimens including a banana tree. The cot's original casters are still intact, meaning it can be wheeled into another part of the loft if required.

The interior of the loft was a big blank canvas, with bare walls and imposing concrete beamed ceilings set within a beautiful architectural framework, and offered Louise plenty of potential for creative thinking when it came to designing and decorating her space. The loft needed to be divided into areas for living, sleeping and working but, conscious that she didn't want to lose the sense of airiness or the industrial aesthetic, Louise resisted overly compartmentalizing the interior. The space was large enough to allow for a three-bedroomed apartment, yet the indulgence of the open-plan feel was too much to forsake. Therefore, with the help of an architect, she devised a layout that retained the expansive feel of the space while incorporating a lounge area, kitchen and study plus a raised sleeping area and a large bathroom. Having spent several years living in New York, Louise had plenty of experience of loft living and knew instinctively what would work and what wouldn't. Her sleeping area is compact, but was cleverly designed to include a dressing area too. The majority of the interior was devoted to a soaring open-plan kitchen, dining and living space that utilizes the expanse of the factory's metal-framed windows and fully embraces the concept of loft living.

The real beauty of this loft lies in the interior design and the quirks and eccentricities of some of the chosen pieces. As an interior designer, Louise expends much time and energy sourcing original and custom-made furniture and accessories for her clients. She keeps some of her best finds for her own space, which is home to a constantly evolving mix of utilitarian designs, original Art Deco items and fanciful bohemian pieces too. One of her favourite features is the tiling in the kitchen area, where patterned blue-and-white ceramic tiles cover the floor and extend part-way up the wall, effectively demarcating the cooking and dining area without the need for a physical divider.

ABOVE Louise's bohemian touches have extended to the bathroom, where a cabinet containing different types of glassware, from ornate coloured tumblers to champagne coupes, sits in the far corner. The space has an air of relaxed, feminine elegance, with the curvaceous contemporary bathtub and warm brass fixtures. The towel rail is suitably Art Deco in style, and adds an additional touch of finesse.

RIGHT Teaming original elements with an owner's personal style is what makes loft and warehouse homes such fascinating places. Being able to position decorative objects alongside the functional workings of an ex-industrial space can create a delightful end result. Here, old plumbing and pipework sit quite comfortably alongside a shapely mirror and wood and glass wall light.

The loft is a haven of eclectic, imaginative ideas, from the vintage wrought-iron cot/crib used as an unusual planter to the idiosyncratic mix of accessories in the living space, where a stuffed bear head, hanging kimono and fringed lantern bring visual interest to the vast open-plan space. The real delight here, however, is Louise's collection of authentic Art Deco furniture and accessories, which allows the space to retain a sense of its own identity while adding a dash of glamour. The Art Deco period is remembered as a golden age of craft, innovation and imagination, and these pieces speak the same confident architectural language as the factory building itself.

FAR LEFT AND LEFT Anouk has introduced some simple but sumptuous textures and colours. The sofa has been upholstered in corduroy, a durable, velvety fabric that softens with age, and the soft grey colour adds a dash of boho luxury when teamed with a tactile sheepskin throw. Repurposed shiny black gin bottles nearby make unusual candleholders.

BELOW Contemporary lighting designs are ideal for bringing an understated yet luxurious element to a raw architectural backdrop. Inspired by the classic chandelier, this modern piece consists of an angular construction of metal rods fitted with simple bare round bulbs and elegantly combines form and function.

OPPOSITE The clean lines and smooth surface of the central cube create a stark contrast to the rugged, uneven configuration of the exposed brickwork, adding textural interest to the decor. Large open-plan interiors often benefit from spatial remodelling and here the living room has a nicely contained feel while still being connected to the rest of the ground floor.

THE BOHEMIAN BAKERY

TRANSFORMING AN EX-RETAIL UNIT INTO a residential space can require a more radical approach than one might expect. To create a home that is architecturally compelling both inside and out sometimes involves the total reconstruction of a bland shop facade. What this former bakery on the outskirts of Amsterdam originally lacked in kerb appeal it made up for in size, and it is now a generously proportioned and stylish family home.

For Anouk Pruim and her husband Andries, undertaking extensive modifications to the exterior of the bakery seemed like the right thing to do. The interior was divided into a shop area with a counter and shelves at the front and a small industrial kitchen at the back where the bread and cakes were baked. While it had been in operation as a bakery for

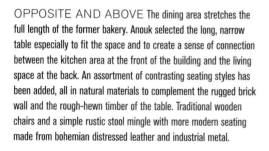

OPPOSITE AND ABOVE The dining area stretches the full length of the former bakery. Anouk selected the long, narrow table especially to fit the space and to create a sense of connection between the kitchen area at the front of the building and the living space at the back. An assortment of contrasting seating styles has been added, all in natural materials to complement the rugged brick wall and the rough-hewn timber of the table. Traditional wooden chairs and a simple rustic stool mingle with more modern seating made from bohemian distressed leather and industrial metal.

as long as the family could remember, old photographs from the 19th century showed that the building had started its life as two separate houses. The charming monochrome images revealed that the pair of dwellings shared the same vernacular as neighbouring properties, with their flat-fronted brick facades, gabled roofs and simple windows and doors.

Somewhere during the transformation from residential use to retail space the original aesthetic of the building had

disappeared and all that remained was a vast floor space that had once been two separate houses. The couple could see plenty of potential for a sizeable family home as well as a separate office for Anouk in the annexe at the rear of the property. Aware that the exterior needed redesigning and the entire interior space required complete reconfiguration and rebuilding, the couple employed the services of local architect and neighbour Joost de Haan. His sympathetic approach, combined with some

ABOVE Roughly luxurious, the living area seamlessly fuses industrial-inspired decorative finishes such as concrete, wood and plaster with sumptuous textiles and rich patterns in an understated palette of colours. The main wall has been treated with Coristil, a slaked lime and marble powder mix that creates a polished feel similar to bare plaster but with a decorative golden hue. It is a pleasingly natural and tactile alternative to modern paint finishes.

clever spatial ideas, has resulted in a distinctive home that spans three floors and utilizes the vast loft space that exists at the top of the building.

Downstairs, the architect incorporated a large square structure into the centre of the open-plan area to house the stairwell, a cloakroom, storage cupboards and an inset fireplace in the living area. This structure also allowed a significant expanse of ceiling to be opened to the upper level, creating a large lightwell that illuminates the ground floor. This central cube also divides up what would otherwise be a massive open space so that the living area is nicely tucked away from the kitchen but the two spaces are linked by a wide corridor-style spaces on either side. One leads from the front door past the downstairs cloakroom to the living area, while the other is home to a sociable dining area, connecting with the kitchen at the front and leading to glass doors at the far end that open onto the courtyard and Anouk's home office. The generous proportions of the space have been fully utilized to great effect, with an

ABOVE The kitchen is an essay in successfuly combining old and new to create an effortlessly restrained while sophisticated look. Dark and luxurious, the space features a host of beautiful yet functional materials and accessories. Modern wenge wood cabinets, the marron emperador marble worktop and contemporary metallic pendant lights offer a sublime contrast to the equally inspiring time-worn rustic elements.

OPPOSITE The battered brick wall provides a visual narrative of the bakery's industrial past, and its warm terracotta hues set the tone for the rest of the rough-luxe elements. A solidly built vintage carpenter's bench delivers a chunky element of industrial chic and is nicely complemented by a frayed antique kelim rug and a pair of utilitarian metal garbage bins.

impressive 8-metre/26-foot galley kitchen situated at the front of the building and a long, narrow 6-metre/20-foot dining table that provides ample eating space as well as plenty of room for the children to do their homework.

Anouk has been ingenious in her use of colours and materials, contrasting scarred brick and worn wood with sleek surfaces, gleaming metals and modern styles as well as shades of both light and dark. The finished look is what the interiors world describes as 'rough luxe': a sublime and desirable amalgamation of the rough and the luxurious. Anouk has taken urban pioneering to sophisticated new heights in this converted bakery, maximizing the visual impact of the original structure and contrasting it with some carefully chosen new additions. The haphazard patchwork brick wall in the kitchen, for example, bears many scars of former construction work yet works perfectly alongside the clean-lined kitchen cabinets and polished marble worksurface.

Similarly, in the living space, the large wall behind the seating area has been finished with Coristil for a subtle but highly modern look. Made from slaked lime and marble powders, this robust wall covering provides a polished concrete-like finish in a sleek golden

OPPOSITE AND ABOVE The building's pitched roof provides the master bedroom with character. The furniture is arranged to fit around the differing ceiling heights in this large space, with the bed strategically positioned under the slope of the room to benefit from the light from the nearby window. The walls were clad in sheets of plywood and stained a rich brown hue to give the space a cosy intimacy despite its cavernous proportions. Task lights make attractive bedside lamps and are teamed with linen in deep jewel shades for some classic urban boho style.

RIGHT A mid-height partition wall divides the ensuite bathroom from the master bedroom. Anouk covered it with the same matt black finish as the central cube in the downstairs living area for continuity. Old-fashioned Bakelite-style light switches sit alongside elegant contemporary wall lights and modern wall-mounted taps/faucets. An old wooden chest of drawers has been given a new lease of life as a vanity unit and holds a beautiful burnished copper sink with plenty of storage space underneath.

LEFT A woven kelim runner is a plush addition to any space and provides warmth underfoot. Its length serves to visually link the bathroom with a dressing area at the other end. Here, Anouk has used simple utilitarian metal garment rails on casters that neatly tuck under the sloping ceilings and make the most of what would otherwise be redundant space.

ABOVE AND OPPOSITE Ex-workplace staples such as metal storage lockers, task lamps and functional chairs add some utility chic to an interior. Anouk has also collected various vintage pieces for her home office, which is situated in the adjoining annexe (opposite). A factory chair, old school chair and mesh storage bring industrial charm to this eclectic space.

hue that beautifully complements the matt black shade on the exterior of the central cube along with the slubby bohemian textiles, softly distressed leather and eclectic industrial pieces that furnish the living area. Anouk decided to introduce these deep, dark shades and rich textures to provide some definition in what would otherwise have been a very large, light space. In the couple's master bedroom and ensuite bathroom at the very top of the house, a similar effect has been created using functional sheets of plywood. These have been used to line the walls and ceiling, but they are elevated beyond the ordinary thanks to the application of a lustrous chestnut-brown wood stain. This shimmers as it catches the light, adding as it does so another layer of depth and intrigue to this dramatically raw yet luxurious interior.

OPPOSITE AND BELOW The galley kitchen beneath the mezzanine is both visually enhancing and practical, with a combination of simple panelled cabinets and open shelves. The island successfully conceals essential appliances, while the extended wood worksurface creates a breakfast bar for relaxed dining.

RIGHT Classic utilitarian clip-top glass jars offer airtight storage for dry foodstuffs and make an interesting display. Floating shelves are a great way of adding stylish storage to an open-plan kitchen – their simple design provides the ideal surface for everyday items.

FAR RIGHT An old factory trolley holds a collection of vintage jars. the green-tinged glass of which is enhanced by the pastel tones in the peeling plaster wall behind. Original wall finishes uncovered during a restoration are worth hanging on to. Seal them with a watered-down PVA solution to protect the surface.

SCHOOL HOUSE CHIC

CONVERTING A FORMER MUNICIPAL OR INDUSTRIAL space into a domestic residence relies on more than just an architectural intervention. When part of this old school building in Amsterdam came up for sale, it did not have planning permission for a change of use to residential. The owners were undeterred, however – the attraction of this unique building was so great that they bought it regardless.

Fortunately, permission for a conversion was granted and the space – former classrooms and school gymnasium, split over two levels – is now a stunning home that marries the old and the new. What makes it even more charming is that the remaining school buildings are still in use, so the chatter of children in the playground can be heard at break times.

The school house is certainly testament to the belief that old buildings were constructed with more strength and skill than their modern-day counterparts, and also with greater attention to detail, which is often the key attraction for urban pioneers looking for spaces to convert into unusual homes. The proportions of the building are magnificent and so too are the architectural details, such as the large windows, the high ceilings and the wooden structural beams that have been left unpainted. At the time of purchase, the school house was in an abandoned state and the original gymnasium fixtures and fittings were still intact. The owners, Thomas and Bibi, retained them to add charm and authenticity to the interior and to bring character to their new home.

As the gymnasium had most of the pulling power aesthetically speaking, it made sense to invert the conventional configuration of living and sleeping spaces and so the classrooms downstairs were made into large bedrooms with raised levels for storage and a luxurious family bathroom. The internal corridor and original staircase that links the two floors have been preserved and a sturdy old school sink once used

ABOVE AND BELOW LEFT
A mezzanine level is a practical design addition to a high-ceilinged space such as this former school gymnasium and offers a sensational viewing platform from which to admire the interior's architecturally distinctive features. Bibi and Thomas have created a characterful home office here, tucked away from the main living space, and accessorized it with a long desk, vintage factory stools and other quirky workplace curios.

OPPOSITE Retaining the old gymnasium equipment has added bags of authentic character and charm to the living area – the pommel horse, hanging ropes and wall-mounted climbing frames are all prized original features. The couple also preserved the gym floor with its slightly worn white markings. It is a wonderful utilitarian backdrop for Bibi's bohemian touches, such as the organic glass pendants, the sparkly accessories and the global textiles and artefacts.

THIS PAGE Creating a homely feel in a vast space can be challenging, but Bibi and Thomas have imbued their home with a relaxed, casual feel. The daybed, sofa and armchairs are generously sized and adorned with plenty of comfy scatter cushions in a myriad of eye-catching colours and designs. And not one but three large log baskets, piled high with wood, are lined up against the wall, hinting at what to look forward to in the colder months.

by the schoolchildren and positioned halfway up the stairs has become a quirky home for houseplants.

Upstairs, a mezzanine level was added to the gymnasium space to accommodate a home office accessed via hidden stairs behind the kitchen area. These continue up to a sizeable roof terrace at the top of the building. The gym is a vast expanse, but the metal and rope pulley system suspended from the ceiling provides a much-needed focal point and draws the eye down, visually lowering the ceiling height without losing the lofty feel. The area has been meticulously planned to make the most of the light and the sense of space. Interiors on an industrial scale can be daunting and, if not structured carefully, can feel empty and exposed. The secret is to divide the space into separate zones that remain linked in some way. Here, the

ABOVE The white walls of the main space allow the architectural features of the structure, such as the natural wood beams, steel supports and the mechanics of the ceiling-mounted gym equipment, to stand out and be admired.

FAR LEFT The wall-mounted climbing frames are accentuated by the couple's books and artworks, displayed on specially constructed shelving with cupboards beneath.

LEFT A simple ball of string stored in a rustic seedlings tray adds a dash of relaxed style. Elements of the natural world are essential to provide visual respite from an urban setting, and even some simple gardening equipment can offer a subliminal connection to nature.

kitchen has been designated an informal social hub with plenty of space for cooking and food prep, and its position under the mezzanine makes it feel something of a cosy nook. The decor is fittingly robust and utilitarian, with classic Shaker-style cabinetry topped with a reclaimed timber worksurface-cum-breakfast bar, display shelving, old factory chairs repurposed as bar stools and a trolley on casters offering additional storage. Various textural nuances have been retained, including the original gym floor with its time-worn markings, and a section of peeling plaster wall reveals pastel hues that visually balance the space's structural elements in iron and wood.

Against all of this, Bibi has introduced many delicate decorative touches that enhance the sense of light and space and bring an eclectic, bohemian mood to the interior. A collection of vintage glass bottles and antique silverware makes a great display, and bulbous blown-glass lights hang low over the dining table, catching a twinkle of light from an oversized mirror. Textiles add warmth and interest, ranging from natural fur to soft velvet and encompassing global patterns such as ikat, batik and woven kelims. These sit happily alongside rustic baskets piled high with logs for the fire. Then of course there is the scattering of houseplants: gloriously oversized specimens in huge pots and smaller ones massed together in a glass terrarium for a lovely slice of boho jungle.

ABOVE Bibi and Thomas have embraced utility chic in their ensuite shower room. The custom-made steel and glass shower door works perfectly with the traditional Victorian-style showerheads and the cement wall finish. Wall lights with classic filament bulbs and Bakelite switches complete the look. The approach combines the best of modern design with elements of the past in a striking monochrome palette – simple to emulate, and stylish and practical too.

OPPOSITE In contrast to the shower enclosure, Bibi has added plenty of cosy, comforting elements to the master bedroom. There is built-in storage aplenty, much of it concealed behind the room divider-cum-headboard. Large windows ensure the space is flooded with light, and walls are a rich taupe. There are nods to industrial design, but the oversized task lamp and cast-iron bathtub are set among tactile furs, scented candles and embroidered bed linen.

OPPOSITE AND BELOW Gallons of white paint were applied to make this former ship chandlery into a bright and light modern home. In the kitchen, it has created a clean canvas against which Rebecca has added pops of nautical blue and shiny steel. This space has a relaxed feel with a smattering of industrial references including the metal panels on the central island, the old catering food storage units and the red factory stools.

RIGHT Originally produced as downlighters to illuminate factory floors, aluminium pendant lights are an ideal choice for a hallway or kitchen where bright overhead lighting is required. Here one is hung from a hook at the end of an original rope pulley to light up a corner of the loft.

FAR RIGHT A pair of elegant paper and wire lanterns placed on top of the industrial food storage cupboards provides a fanciful decorative touch.

SHIP SHAPE

REDEVELOPING A WAREHOUSE BUILDING requires vision, skill and determination, and the huge proportions and various obstacles involved can be enough to deter even the most enterprising of urban pioneers. However, on New York's waterfront, this former ship chandlery has undergone a remarkable transformation and is now a beautiful home containing many references to its seafaring heritage.

The warehouse is situated in the historic South Street Seaport District of Lower Manhattan, where much of the city's maritime legacy is still evident among the cobblestone streets and brick-built warehouses. As New York's shipping industries thrived here, so too did various associated enterprises.

THIS PAGE The interior was originally two buildings and the longitudinal wooden beams are what remain of the dividing wall. They still provide a sense of separation within the large open-plan space. Their sturdy verticals are echoed nicely in Rebecca's choice of full-length curtains, which provide the white interior with some definition at the far end of the apartment.

THIS PAGE As an interior designer, Rebecca is adept at arranging furniture and accessories to create highly appealing spaces for relaxed living. Here, an interesting mix of seating has been unified with a palette of conservative taupe and grey. To add life and vibrancy, large glossy-leaved houseplants have been introduced.

RIGHT This impressive timber and wooden winch was installed in the building when it was constructed in 1839 and was retained during the renovation. Once used to haul sailcloth and other supplies, it now creates a stunning focal point in the corner of the loft. Retaining historic features such as this one is crucial in achieving a successful conversion and preserving a sense of heritage too.

This five-storey building was constructed in 1839 as an outfitter for sailboats in the nearby dock and was originally two row/terraced buildings that were combined in 1882 to accommodate a bar and brothel with 'entertainment' rooms above. Some years later, the building was incorporated into the nearby wholesale Fulton Fish Market.

When architect/wine merchant Marco and his interior designer wife Rebecca bought the warehouse, the fish market was still operational. The building was a wreck and smelled strongly of fish. But the waterside location, just a few blocks from City Hall and Wall Street and with views over Brooklyn Bridge, won them over.

Despite its derelict state, the building retained evidence of its illustrious past. The original floors were still intact, laid like a ship's deck with pitch-soaked rope between each plank, and on the lower floors, there were barrel marks on the wooden boards. Sails were sewn on the upper floors and the brass markers used to measure the heavy canvas remained. The original staircase, with its worn steps and handrail, was still in place, as were the large wood pillars in the centre of the living space – structural dividers dating back to when the property was two neighbouring buildings.

RIGHT Industrial metal shelves offer storage for the couple's large collection of books and files. A matching set of baskets adds softness and a sense of orderliness as well as providing plenty of space to store Luca's toys and games. Simply woven and with a rustic texture, they have had a modern nautical update with a wraparound layer of white paint, establishing a subtle connection with the white brick wall and timber beams of the interior.

Each floor of the building spans an eyewatering 250 square metres/2700 square feet and much of the space hadn't been touched for over 100 years. To contemplate such a mammoth project requires a strategy and Marco and Rebecca began by restoring the shell, repointing the facade and replacing the windows and the rusting fire escape. Once that was completed, the couple worked on each of the floors in turn, starting at the top with what would eventually be their own home and working their way down. The other lofts would be rentals, while the ground floor was to be the premises for Marco's wine business. The couple blasted the old beams and sanded and pickled the original floors. Key architectural details such as the wood columns and the giant hoist once used to haul sailcloth and other nautical supplies were retained and make a striking visual feature in a corner of the living space.

Rebecca's years of experience as a former home and decorating editor at *Martha Stewart Living* magazine meant she had many ideas for how to maximize the potential of their loft space. The couple needed to section off part of the open-plan interior for bedrooms and a bathroom, but they didn't want to forsake the wonderful sense of space. The solution was a custom-built bookcase that runs the whole width of the loft and divides it into a front living space and a rear suite of bedrooms, storage and bathroom. The former is divided into different zones and consists of a kitchen, dining area, two sitting

OPPOSITE Rebecca works from home, so an alcove at one end of the open-plan space has been turned into a stylish home office. The vintage steel desk enables good organization, while accessories such as the old-fashioned typewriter and industrial clock add playful charm. Marco's racing bikes are suspended on the wall in a functional yet decorative fashion.

RIGHT This wall of bookshelves is a room divider and storage system in one and separates the bedrooms and bathroom from the rest of the open-plan living space. The vintage rolling ladder on casters is attached to a metal rail and slides along to provide access to books at this end of the space, and tableware at the kitchen end.

nooks and a play area for their son. Inspired by the building's history, Rebecca introduced playful references: the Delft tiles on the chimneybreast are a nod to the area's Dutch roots, and the full-length curtains that screen the bright summer sun are in nautical blue and white.

Marco is also a furniture designer and many of his designs, such as the bookcase, sofa, bed and dining table, enjoy centre stage here. They are the perfect complement to Rebecca's antique and vintage pieces, most of them found at the Brimfield Antique Show or websites such as eBay and Etsy. The kitchen was created from old wood found in a nearby building, while the wood cladding in the bedroom and bathroom was salvaged from one of the lower floors. So many pieces here have a story to tell, just like the building itself.

BELOW LEFT The bed is one of Marco's designs and is solidly reassuring in style. A bolster pillow provides old-fashioned charm, with the vintage sequinned wedding blanket striking a bohemian note. Rebecca has made a lovely wall of photos with simple, transparent folders pinned in a rectangular grid to the wooden panelling. This is an ingenious and inexpensive way of displaying family photos and allows for quick and easy updates as and when required.

BELOW RIGHT Natural wood tones in the bedroom furniture contribute welcome warmth. Classic task lamps are utilized for illumination here, and the brass wall-mounted bedside lamps are complemented by this pretty swan-neck design on the vintage bedroom desk.

OPPOSITE The bathroom is indulgent and full of nautical nuances. A luxuriously deep bathtub is adorned with a boldly pattered shower curtain that adds visual impact. Rebecca has introduced plenty of splashes of marine blue.

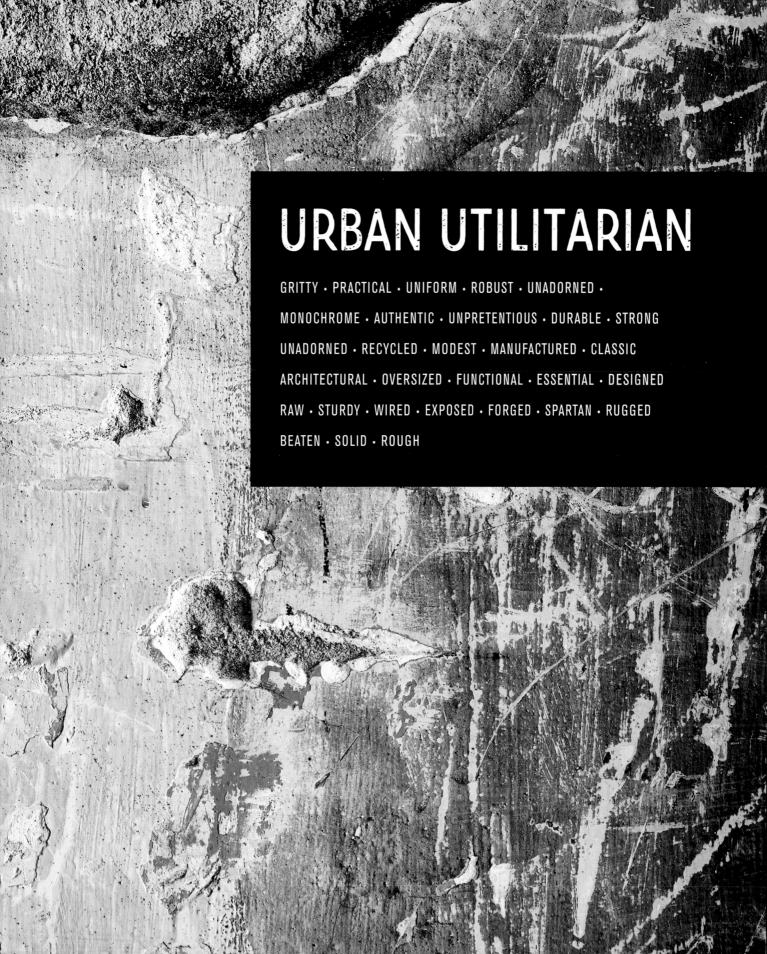

URBAN UTILITARIAN

GRITTY · PRACTICAL · UNIFORM · ROBUST · UNADORNED ·
MONOCHROME · AUTHENTIC · UNPRETENTIOUS · DURABLE · STRONG
UNADORNED · RECYCLED · MODEST · MANUFACTURED · CLASSIC
ARCHITECTURAL · OVERSIZED · FUNCTIONAL · ESSENTIAL · DESIGNED
RAW · STURDY · WIRED · EXPOSED · FORGED · SPARTAN · RUGGED
BEATEN · SOLID · ROUGH

OPPOSITE, RIGHT AND BELOW
Kitchens are practical spaces, so naturally suit many heavy-duty materials and accessories that are instantly recognizable as industrial staples due to their combination of functionality and style. James has combined some of the best ideas for a dramatic overall look, such as classic Shaker-style panelled cabinets, marble worksurfaces, stainless steel canteen-style equipment, metal strip lighting and exposed steel ducting. The floor tiles add decorative detail but are actually just as hardwearing and robust as the steel and reinforced glass. The muddy tones of the peeling plaster wall act as a cohesive colour reference for the other elements in the space.

FAR RIGHT The huge old clock was passed down to James from his father and hangs in pride of place from the kitchen ceiling. James fixed classic tin tiles in a natural metal finish to the ceiling for a further injection of industrial style and a splash of pattern.

UTILITY CHIC

FOR IMAGINATIVE AND EXPERIMENTAL THINKERS like architects and designers, every redundant urban space offers an opportunity for creative endeavour, no matter how unappealing the site might initially appear. In the up-and-coming area of Oost Amsterdam, a garage that lay empty and derelict for more than 20 years has recently been transformed into a quirky, characterful home.

Sitting among the modern terraces of this eastern suburb, far from the picturesque gabled townhouses of central Amsterdam, architect James van der Velden discovered a boarded-up, unused garage that had been abandoned for more than two decades. Built in the early 1900s, the building was a long, rectangular construction of 85 square metres/915 square feet with dank brick walls, decaying doors and no windows.

THIS PAGE The rear part of the former garage was excavated to create a 'well' for the main living space. This configuration works brilliantly – the dining area is connected to the kitchen and is easily accessed via a small flight of steps, but it also feels snug and nicely contained within its own section of floor space.

However, despite its unpromising appearance, James realized that the space could be transformed into a unique home.

The first step towards converting the building into a residential property was the replacement of the garage doors with a large window and door at the front. New windows were inserted at either end of the space and James added internal walls to break up the long, narrow interior and create a kitchen, dining area and living space, two bedrooms and a bathroom, and an office. Digging down into the foundations increased the depth of the interior and created an additional 40 square metres/430 square feet of space, allowing

for a split-level master bedroom and bathroom on a raised floor above the lower-level dining area. A glazed internal room between the dining and living areas accommodates a home office/snug, and a tiny space at the back has been made into a small patio accessed through full-height glass doors – a key light source for the living area. The result is a brilliantly practical living space that's architecturally intriguing too, with contrasting dark and light zones arranged over different levels.

James has opted for a robustly industrial design aesthetic throughout. He kept the walls untouched wherever possible, leaving exposed the builder's marks, crumbling

ABOVE As the former garage wasn't a historic building with any distinguishing architectural features, James started from scratch with a bare shell and designed a living space that is perfectly suited to modern living. He added elements of the industrial aesthetic for visual impact wherever appropriate.

OPPOSITE The living room has been provided with some traditional elements to create a cosy and welcoming mood. A stone fireplace and full-length velvet curtains in a rich mustard bring warmth and comfort to balance the urban feel of the painted brick walls.

LEFT A custom-built shelving unit offers valuable storage space in the living area. It's home to an eclectic array of oil paintings, industrial lights and mechanical instruments, family photos and the couple's vast collection of art books, as well as a menagerie of stuffed birds and zoological curios.

plaster and battered brickwork. As a result, the interior pays tribute to the building's past and is the perfect backdrop for a collection of artefacts, antiques, books, framed photos and other paraphernalia, the majority of which is displayed on a shelving and storage unit that spans the length of the living area.

The raised bedroom and bathroom are positioned above the dining area. Behind a sturdy steel-framed wire-glass wall overlooking the kitchen is the bathroom, where the same materials were used to create a double shower unit. Classic utilitarian fixtures and fittings feature here, including metro tiles, Bakelite switches, bulkhead lighting, factory pendant lights, black slatted factory blinds and a whole host of sturdy, built-to-last architectural ironmongery.

OPPOSITE BELOW The internal cube was designed to create a separate home office. The doors are steel with glazed partitions and painted a smart dark green. The cube also provides the living area at the back of the space with a sense of separation and containment.

ABOVE AND RIGHT Inside the office James has indulged his love of the natural world and historic exploration with a wallpaper mural of palm trees accessorized with vintage suitcases and avian and zoological knicknacks. Industrial references abound here too, such as the black factory-style blinds at the windows, the vintage wooden desk and the Jieldé floor lamp.

In the same vein, the furniture and accessories include an assortment of industrial classics, such as metal factory shelving, professional catering equipment and vintage factory stools in the kitchen, plus wooden storage crates, metal Tolix chairs and a super-sized vintage factory clock. The moody monochrome hues of the decor and the warm brick and plaster walls beautifully complement an eclectic array of curios, which range from vintage suitcases and explorer's specimen jars to oversized light bulbs, bird's eggs, Fornasetti plates and contemporary art. Urban grit and rough-hewn styling are combined with a dash of contemporary gloss and glamour.

James's home is not so much a lesson in how to make the most of the space you have, but how to make something from nothing at all. This disused garage has been given a new life as a luxurious and comfortable home without denying or concealing its past.

OPPOSITE Bathrooms are areas of high moisture and condensation levels, so make sure any lighting fixtures are suitable. James has used a brass bulkhead light on the wall and classic ship's lights on the ceiling. Designed to be robust enough to withstand the elements, both are ideal for adding industrial style and function to bathrooms and shower rooms.

ABOVE LEFT The bathroom is positioned at the very front of the mezzanine level and therefore overlooks the kitchen. For privacy (and some industrial chic), a black Venetian blind is ideal. The patches of rust on the exterior of the reclaimed bathtub add character, as does the peeling plaster wall.

ABOVE RIGHT The walk-in shower oozes utility chic with its steel cubicle doors and wire-mesh glass, metro brick tiles grouted black for definition and monochrome encaustic tiles for the floor. Their decorative pattern implies a little luxury, while also being fittingly austere in style, as does the pair of showers.

RIGHT The bedroom has been afforded a degree of comfort with some unexpected utilitarian references. A charcoal grey suiting wool has been used to cover the headboard and complements the other fabrics. Meanwhile, an elegant wall-mounted industrial task light with a slender metal arm and shapely glass shade makes a neat and stylish reading lamp.

OPPOSITE AND RIGHT The building's wood structure is solidly made and provides plenty of elegance to the interior. The magnificence of the full-height windows and main entrance doors can be fully appreciated from inside the building. Isabelle has used black paint in a high gloss finish for the metal doors, window frames and the radiators, allowing them to act as architectural punctuation marks against the neutral backdrop. She has also hung a chandelier in the hallway and covered it with dried foliage to bring some decorative embellishment to the spartan interior.

BELOW The wooden surface of the hallway cupboards has been sanded down in keeping with the rest of the woodwork, revealing a softly aged patina in the process and highlighting the intricate brass door latches and hinges. The cupboards would have originally been built as lockers for the factory workers to store their personal possessions. Isabelle uses them to hold linens and tablecloths for her events business.

FACTORY FASHION

CONVERTING A FACTORY OR MUNICIPAL UNIT into a home often means a reconfiguration of the internal layout to fully maximize the property's potential for modern living. However, retaining an unusual layout that was specifically designed for industrial operations can sometimes provide the homeowner with a myriad of unexpected opportunities.

Situated in the heart of Paris, down a narrow street in the shadow of the Eiffel Tower, a building that over the years was a thriving hub for various different industries is now a unique live/work and entertaining space. Built towards the middle of the last century, the factory was one of several inner-city electricity supply stations that eventually became part of EDF, France's national electricity company, when it was formed in 1946. This particular building would have been responsible for

LEFT A simple ceramic sink, basic white tiles and a classic French wall-mounted soap holder, designed to ensure the soap is always to hand, make a utilitarian statement in the hallway. It would have provided the workers with a place to freshen up after a shift. Unusual original features such as this are well worth retaining.

BELOW LEFT The original sectioned-off clerk's office at the front of the building is utilized by Isabelle as her office space, from which she runs her fashion and beauty PR business. She has cleverly repurposed the original glass-fronted counter and cubicle behind the partition as a cloakroom. With the addition of a simple steel clothes rail, some basic wooden coat hangers and a large factory pendant light, it is a charming recreation of the factory's past.

OPPOSITE Isabelle has created a relaxed meeting area at one end of the interior. Opting for lightweight wicker chairs and a small vintage table means she can clear the space for events when required. The natural linen curtains screen off the shelving that she uses for storing office supplies and are a simple but effective alternative to cupboard doors. The black wooden ladders provide access to the top shelves as well as acting as a strong decorative statement against the natural wicker and white painted wood.

supplying power to the entire Champs de Mars district in the 7th Arrondissement on Paris's Left Bank. EDF eventually vacated the building, moving their operations to newer premises. Between then and the time that its current owner Isabelle Roque bought it in the mid 1990s, the building was home to various other industries, most notably ORTF (Office de Radiodiffusion-Télévision Française), the national agency that provided the public radio and television in France during the 1960s and 70s.

When Isabelle purchased the property, it retained many of its original features both inside and out. From the pavement, a tall sliding metal gate topped with spiked railings hints at the security measures that would have been a requisite during its time as an electricity supplier. Inside the gate, a pretty cobbled courtyard provides a patch of outside space where Isabelle has arranged a few potted plants to create a small urban oasis. Leafy shrubs, evergreens and climbing varieties offer a bit of untamed nature and soften the building's concrete, brick and metal exterior.

The building is entered via a tall metal double door and lofty rectangular glass-panelled windows painted a nondescript off-white that plays down their architectural impact. The inside of these doors and windows, however, has been coated in a glossy jet black, which brings the pencil-thin verticals of the window frames greater prominence and definition. This acts as an important lesson to

RIGHT AND FAR RIGHT Deep box files are well used and well worn, with much workplace history ingrained in the peeling surfaces and frayed edges. The original floor still exists and bears the scars of previous use. The painted sections would have marked out specific work zones, and over the years have been rubbed way. What remains on show holds a lot of aesthetic appeal.

BELOW The atelier contains some spectacular original lighting. This elegant suspended pendant would once have illuminated the factory floor below. Designs such as these are highly sought after as style statements for modern interiors.

those wanting to restore an industrial space – sometimes an interior's most uninspiring architectural detail can, with the appropriate creative treatment, end up becoming one of its most distinctive.

Of course, this is Paris, the capital city of a country that is synonymous with style. As far as industrial design goes, attention to detail comes in bucketloads, as many iconic French designs that are treasured today can verify. These designs are often revered as much for their form as for their function, and this former workplace has plenty of such examples. The cast-iron radiators have slender, attenuated ribs, classic factory pendant shades are elegantly suspended from wall-mounted steel arcs and a wall of wooden storage lockers has robust panelled detailing with ornate brass latches.

OPPOSITE Isabelle has enhanced the building's finest features and resisted making any structural changes or remodelling the internal layout. The central staircase and wooden internal office are solidly constructed and were evidently built to last.

L'EAU QUI FAIT *pschitt*..

THIS PAGE The simple, elegant kitchen is strategically positioned on the mezzanine level by the front windows. It is a generously sized space for cooking and entertaining. Against a soft taupe background, black, white and stainless steel elements combine to create a classic uniform for the urban utilitarian kitchen. Functional in form and with a sharp, monochrome aesthetic, it provides practicality in abundance. Isabelle has added a super-sized spun aluminium pendant light for some iconic French factory flair.

Isabelle's home is very much still the utilitarian space it once was. The original factory floor is dominated by a wide entrance hall and central staircase leading up to two mezzanine levels. To many, it might have made sense to demolish the imposing internal divisions and opt for a more traditional domestic layout. For Isabelle, however, the interior offered the possibility of an unconventional and versatile abode. She has gradually created a home in and around the original layout, configuring a dining and cooking space on one side of the mezzanine, and a bedroom and living area on the other.

The space could be described as Isabelle's atelier, where she lives and from which she runs a successful PR and events company. Visiting clients were often enchanted with the space and gradually, one by one, asked to use it for events. Now Isabelle lets out the ground floor as a venue and photographic location, and the original factory floor has once again come into its own. The wooden internal room to the far side of the ground floor provides storage for chairs and trestle tables that are pulled out as and when needed. The area tucked away at the back is a relaxed meeting place for clients, with concealed storage for work

ABOVE LEFT The kitchen is fashionably simple and utilitarian, in keeping with the pared-back feel of the rest of the interior. Isabelle has combined vintage industrial pieces with natural elements that resonate with the wooden features of this spartan factory interior. A vintage school bench by the window holds shapely wicker and rush baskets. They are practical containers, but with their intricate woven form and natural tones, they add a touch of decorative aesthetic too and some soft texture.

ABOVE RIGHT For the kitchen, Isabelle sourced workplace classics such as these machinist chairs and factory stool. Fabric panels were stitched from natural linen and pinned to the wooden mezzanine structure. The vast ceiling height can be fully appreciated from this angle. The rope pulley system was devised to open and close overhead skylights that otherwise would be out of reach.

ABOVE Open-plan storage brings an element of orderliness where serveware and objects of use can be instantly located. Like the workings of a factory, kitchen essentials such as plates and bowls can all be neatly stacked in regimental rows to make the process of taking out and putting away run like clockwork. Isabelle has amassed a collection of simple and practical staples such as Duralex glassware and white canteen plates.

RIGHT Perched high up in the mezzanine level, internal windows provide a connection with Isabelle's living space and the rest of the factory. The natural tones that run throughout have been spruced up in this private part of the work/live unit with an intense burst of rich orange fabric on the daybed. The pop of colour isn't overbearing but is just enough to highlight the warmth in the wood and accent the orange in the artwork just seen in the kitchen opposite.

supplies behind the utility-style linen curtains hung from a simple wooden pole. And the large expanses of wall can be used as a screen for presentations.

This is a vast and somewhat spartan space, but it is full of history and character. Instead of adapting the space to meet her needs, Isabelle has cleverly adapted both herself and her work to make the most of this unique space and to allow it to reach its full potential.

LEFT Minimal and modern, the clean lines on show in the kitchen recur throughout this serene space. The slender metal table base, the curved wooden detail of the bentwood dining chairs and even the sleek stainless steel handles on the refrigerator act as architectural silhouettes to provide a sense of space and calm.

BELOW Attention to detail is paramount when creating a successful minimal interior. Considered use of materials and clever design of internal structures can produce one that is successful at all levels. Here, the staircase that joins the ground floor with the upper level incorporates the pared-down but refined aesthetic used throughout. White oak ply and black metal tubing are elevated to a luxurious level by the sharp angular construction.

OASIS OF CALM

JUDGE THIS URBAN BUILDING in Brooklyn, New York, by its undistinguished brick and metal facade, and you might safely assume that it was just a humble garage. But while the space behind the aluminium roller shutters is indeed used to store a car, enter through the graffiti-covered metal grille door to the left and you will discover a truly remarkable domestic transformation.

Built around 1930, the building started life as a feather factory, then became a storage space for an automobile parts business. When architects Philipp and Kit von Dalwig discovered the place, there was little evidence left of either usage, just a dilapidated abandoned building with broken windows and skylights. Sandwiched between Brooklyn's residential brownstones and an industrial suburb, the block

THIS PAGE The kitchen is plain and practical with an artisanal flavour. Plywood cabinets, stainless steel appliances and marble worksurfaces are interspersed with artful, handcrafted pieces that still conform to the form and function dictate of utilitarian style. The kitchen island, designed by Philipp and Kit, consists of a thin powder-coated steel frame that supports a thick marble slab top.

where the garage is located contains several other former commercial spaces, many of which have been converted into studios and homes in recent years as the area has gained in popularity.

Everything about the couple's home is testament to the idea of simplicity, and their conversion of the garage is a lesson in developing an urban space in a way that is as organic as possible and in tune with the 'slow living' movement at the forefront of contemporary architecture, design and lifestyle thinking. Philipp and Kit wanted both the design process and their finished home to reflect their professional methodology, and the result is a study in

LEFT AND ABOVE Widely used in old-fashioned sculleries and commercial canteens, marble is a favourite for utilitarian kitchens. The accessories here combine practicality with elegance – hardware-store metal brackets, a kitchen tap/faucet with pull-out hose and a clip-on task light. Stacking earthenware bowls with plates that double up as lids, canteen-style tumblers and Pyrex bowls are also pure and simple.

OPPOSITE Philipp and Kit designed the dining table using old pine beams found in upstate New York. With its solid proportions and rich wood tones, the table creates a striking focal point in the open-plan kitchen and living space, and acts as a divider between the two zones. Classic Thonet No. 18 bentwood café chairs, originally designed by German furniture maker Michael Thonet in 1876 for use in restaurants and cafés, make an elegant commercial reference.

space and proportion combined with a thoughtful, refined use of simple, utilitarian materials to create a bright and beautiful family home.

Originally a single-level construction, the main part of the garage has been converted into an open-plan kitchen, living and dining space with a guest room-cum-home office and library at the rear. The original wooden ceiling was restored and left exposed, as were the remaining metal hooks and braces, which act as a reminder of the building's previous modest existence and contribute intricate structural detail to the all-white scheme. Similarly, a heavy-duty metal door at the back of the home office was retained as an architectural token of the building's past. Like the ceiling, it has been given a unifying coat of white paint to seamlessly blend with the rest of the interior.

OPPOSITE TOP LEFT The central patio is visible from the main living space, the office at the back and from the adjoining corridor. This indoor oasis provides a much-needed connection with nature and allows additional daylight into the interior. It is a calm and uncluttered place with a simple planting scheme that contributes an element of quiet, restful contemplation.

OPPOSITE TOP RIGHT The living area is a symphony of style and simplicity. A boxy grey sofa with its clean lines brings visual structure to the all-white interior, while a delicate fringed mohair throw in the softest shell pink provides warmth and comfort. The skinny task lamp adds a contemporary minimal feel.

OPPOSITE BELOW The shelves in the home office are made from thin sheets of aluminium formed into angular constructions and wall mounted. They are ideal for holding files and other everyday bits and paperwork. The Artemide Tolomeo table lamp is a stylish addition.

RIGHT Kit and Philipp have maintained a monochrome scheme throughout for a refined and simple overall aesthetic, and the home office-cum-guest room is no exception. Slender black picture frames casually propped up against the wall cleverly highlight the graphic black-and-white striped design of the bed throw.

One of the most striking components of the main living space is the glass-encased internal courtyard garden. This was created by converting one of the garage's original skylights into a lightwell that not only brings light and air to the heart of the space but also creates a natural divide between the living area and the office/guest room. Thanks to this courtyard, the living space is washed with sunlight and shadows that bounce around the white walls. It also provides a subliminal link to the natural materials used throughout, the most striking of which is the white oak plywood flooring – a step up from the basic ply that is typically used by designers and architects to create a clean, simple finish. The couple also tweaked the brickwork by applying a very thin layer of plaster to the walls to refine the surface while retaining the texture of the brick. This attention to detail has resulted in the serene and calm mood that pervades their home.

A second level was added to the building and this houses two bedrooms and a family bathroom. Accessed by an angular metal and oak staircase, the upper floor continues the tranquil mood played out at ground level. Pristine white walls and pale plywood floors are the backdrop to a smattering of carefully curated design classics. Architects and designers know all too well the power of a restrained monochrome palette in a minimal interior, particularly when it is offset with tones of unfinished wood and clean metal. It's a case of less is more in terms of visual effect, with softness and warmth added in the form of natural textures, materials and light.

The former commercial space has been brought alive with a host of classic pieces, each revered for its design and successful combination of form and function. These provide a feast for the eye but without being in any way showy. Key items include sculptural bentwood chairs by Thonet, slender cantilevered Tolomeo task lights from Artemide and a collection of Alvar Aalto stackable stools, which double as side tables throughout this simple but beautiful converted home.

RIGHT Less is often more when it comes to design. The same restrained use of colours and materials continues in the bedrooms. Against an all-white backdrop, iconic designs such as this Bestlite wall lamp are used as punctuation marks. This celebrated task light, designed by Robert Dudley Best and inspired by the Bauhaus movement, is just as popular today as when it was first manufactured in the 1930s, and demonstrates how just a single industrial element can create an impact.

RIGHT The bathroom also combines practicality and functionality with simplicity and good design. Although plain and minimally decorated, it has a calm, tranquil air and blends with the rest of the interior thanks to its pared-down colour palette. An all-white scheme is interrupted only by a single black stripe in the floor design and the shiny stainless steel showerhead. The pipework has been completely concealed out of sight.

THIS PAGE The guest room is playful in style with a combination of forms. The original metal ladder provides a workplace reference to the building's former use and a place to clip the utility lamp. Comfortable textures are introduced, as well as an indoor swing for the couple's daughter Marlowe. The Prismatic Table by Isamu Noguchi was inspired by the geometric forms of Japanese paperfolding techniques and makes an eye-catching example of a 'form meets function' furniture piece.

OPPOSITE AND RIGHT The imposing structural beams are monumental in proportion and provide the building with a magnificent historical and visual reference point. They create a natural division within the interior, delineating an area for the kitchen, with the space behind used for daughter Lola's raised bedroom. Mark has sourced a pair of ex-factory lamps of industrial dimensions to add drama and highlight the scale of the timber beams.

BELOW Simple and industrial in style, the table is constructed from rusty metal trusses with an old train carriage/car floor as the top. Its rough aesthetic is beautifully contrasted with a collection of elegantly shaped vintage Eames office chairs. The classic Eiffel DSR, with its distinctive metal base, sits alongside ones on casters and adds an alternative industrial reference.

WAREHOUSE WORK OF ART

THIS CENTURIES-OLD WAREHOUSE in central Amsterdam has undergone many changes of use since its construction in 1631. Originally built as a brewery, it has experienced incarnations as a fire station, a Lutheran church and finally a squat before being rescued by its current owners. Today, it is not only an inspiring and idiosyncratic living space but also a busy gallery where up-and-coming contemporary artists display their work.

Dating back over 300 years, the building is situated on Brouwersgracht, or The Brewer's Canal. Deemed by many to be the prettiest canal in central Amsterdam, it is characterized by crooked, narrow buildings, many of them with ornate gables. Marking the northern border of the city's canal ring, Brouwersgracht served as a route for ships from the East carrying silks, spices and other exotic cargos to store in the vast warehouses bordering the water. With good access to large fresh water shipments, the canal also became a popular site for breweries.

Despite being subject to some radical changes of use over the centuries, when owners Mark Chalmers and partner Bianca bought the warehouse it retained much of its original structure. Consisting of an internal space of 190 square metres/2045 square feet, the building is entered through a pair of imposing arched double

LEFT Mark and Bianca's historic warehouse home provides an industrial backdrop for their unique contemporary art collection. The grey robot sculpture that stands sentinel against the timber beam in the living space is entitled '4ft Dissected Companion' by Brooklyn-based artist Kaws. In contrast, a practical and utilitarian large wooden dresser/hutch or *werkplaatskast* by Piet Hein Eek stands at one side of the kitchen.

OPPOSITE ABOVE The ingenious design of daughter Lola's raised bedroom pod has created valuable storage underneath while providing a sense of separation from the main space. The walls are constructed from heavy-duty industrial metal and reinforced glass, and inside a vintage work desk and a factory machinist chair make a quirky workstation for school studies.

OPPOSITE BELOW Open-plan metal shelving provides functional storage in the kitchen. In tough stainless steel, and crammed with catering pots and pans, it also offers storage space for other cookware essentials.

doors that opens into an area that would originally have been a carriage house. From here, a long corridor leads to the living area, which is revealed through a brick archway that frames the space magnificently. Living in a building where history is etched into every beam and mark on the floor means that for Mark, Bianca and their daughter Lola, there is always a sense of occasion when returning home.

Mark is a trained architect and could see that the warehouse had the potential to become a unique family home. Keen to achieve the best results

possible while meeting the requirements of strict building regulations, he employed local architect Stef Bakke to assist with the design. The building is situated within a UNESCO World Heritage Site and is protected by national and municipal heritage listing, so there were restrictions on both internal and external modifications.

THIS PAGE Art and living exist in unison here, all against a backdrop of industrial heritage that dates back centuries. The living room is gallery-like, with art on every surface. Pieces on the wall include 'Star Spangled Shadows' and 'Bunny Boy' by Faile, 'Liquidated Chanel' by Zevs and 'Heron Head' by ROA. On the table, sculptures by contemporary artists such as Parra, Banksy, Medicom and Faile sit side by side.

The warehouse is a large square with soaring 4.5-metre/15-feet ceilings and stripped wooden beams, so a dark concrete floor was added to ground the space and give it definition. The bedrooms are raised on a platform and screened by metal-framed wired-glass walls that provide privacy at the same time as retaining a sense of openness. All the materials used are suitably industrial, with steel, glass, metal and concrete seamlessly blending with the original timber and brick structure. The result is a practical home with essential modern comforts such as underfloor heating and a cast-iron gas stove that heats the whole space and provides a wonderful focal point, especially during the winter.

In creating their utilitarian-style interior, Mark and Bianca have chosen furniture to play a major part, with some oversized, ex-industrial pieces balancing out the tall ceilings. Huge metal lights salvaged from a Polish factory are suspended above a dining table constructed from the base of an old train carriage/car and some rusted steel trusses, and in the kitchen, a large Piet Hein Eek dresser/hutch holds everything from cutlery/flatware and china to DIY tools – it's a functional workhorse that provides plenty of storage while bringing a note of warmth and tradition to the space.

Juxtaposed against all of this is Mark's collection of contemporary street art by celebrated names such as Parra, Banksy, Faile and Daniel Arsham. Propped up against the walls and on every surface, paintings and pieces of sculpture have taken up residence among the vintage and industrial items. Large wooden storage crates have been remodelled into a display unit that holds other pieces. The former carriage house has been given the same

makeover as the rest of the building and is now known as The Garage – a gallery space that celebrates the works of emerging international artists.

Art and everyday life happily coexist here against a backdrop of industrial heritage. As far as Mark is concerned, the building has been standing for many centuries and will be for many more, while he, Bianca and Lola are just the current custodians. He has converted the interior into residential accommodation as simply as possible in order to create a versatile living space that will suit his family for as long as they have the privilege of living here.

ABOVE AND BELOW Rusty tin boxes and the rough wooden drawers of a recycled workbench add time-worn charm that resonates with the building itself. They also provide a refreshing contrast to the contemporary materials in the art. Hanging above the bench is 'Heron Head' by celebrated street artist ROA. Known for applying his work to urban brick exterior facades, it seems fitting that it should find a home inside an urban enclave of modern art such as this.

THIS PAGE The living space at the back of the warehouse is bright and airy and leads onto a patio garden. A large chandelier catches the light from outside, and acts as a decorative contrast to the hefty wood coffee table on industrial casters. On a similar note, a pair of upholstered mid-century chairs provides elegance and the perfect accompaniment to the large comfy sofa.

BELOW Shattered mirror artworks with brass bullets and antique brass frames by international artist Pryce Lee are hung throughout the space. This example, entitled 'Single Shot' with antique bronze, is on display in the open-plan living area, and another is in Lola's bedroom and used as a dressing mirror.

OPPOSITE AND BELOW LEFT Despite Mark's collection of vibrant modern art, the apartment still has a utilitarian feel. Simple light fittings exist alongside a vintage industrial storage cabinet in the main bedroom, which also benefits from the steel and reinforced glass partitions that feature elsewhere in the interior. The bathroom consists of basic white ceramic tiles and a simple linen curtain hung from a metal pole, allowing the rough patina and texture of the structural beams to be the star attraction.

ABOVE In the hallway that leads from the front entrance through the gallery space and into the main living area, a leather jacket hangs casually among stored furniture pieces and framed prints. It is another artwork and part of an installation entitled 'Le Punk Français' by French artist Ludo. This historic building is constantly being updated with new pieces from emerging contemporary artists.

SOURCES

UK & EUROPE

FURNITURE AND ACCESSORIES

Abigail Ahern
abigailahern.com
Furniture and decorative accessories in a sophisticated urban palette of dark hues, sleek metals and industrial tones. Great range of faux flowers and jungly plants.

Anthropologie
Anthropologie.eu
Emporium of colourful, crafted bohemian-style furniture, accessories and kitchenware. UK & US.

The Conran Shop
conranshop.co.uk
Source of extensive range of industrial design classics, including Tolix, Eames and Emeco Navy chairs and contemporary furniture and accessories.

Dyke and Dean
dykeanddean.com
Eclectic mix of classic industrial-inspired utilitarian products, including furniture, bathroom accessories, lighting and kitchenware.

House Doctor
Housedoctor.dk
Danish utility-style furniture and accessories for everyday living. Classics include metal lockers, storage trolleys, refectory tables, canvas storage, bohemian wicker furniture and factory-inspired lighting.

Labour and Wait
labourandwait.co.uk
One-stop shop for timeless functional objects from brooms and brushes to enamelware and Swiss army blankets.

Muji
muji.eu
Practical storage, wood furniture and accessories in utilitarian canvas, metal, chambray and stainless steel for an organized home with a simple, pared-down Japanese aesthetic.

Objects of Use
objectsofuse.com
Beautifully made, enduring household tools and functional items that are a pleasure to use and will last a lifetime.

Rockett St George
rockettstgeorge.co.uk
Online emporium offering covetable industrial-inspired furniture, storage, home accessories, lighting, rugs and photographic brick, concrete and tin tile wallpapers.

LIGHTING

Davey Lighting
davey-lighting.co.uk
Original British marine lighting manufacturer founded in East India Docks in 1880s and recently purchased by Original BTC (see below). Classic nautical exterior and interior styles, including bulkhead lights, mast lights and ships deck lights in a range of robust finishes including weathered brass and copper.

Dowsing and Reynolds
dowsingandreynolds.com
Suppliers of modern and vintage-style lighting components and filament bulbs, including wide range of hip hardware from designer light switches and sockets to industrial-inspired wall clocks.

Original BTC
originalbtc.com
Innovative and classic British-designed and manufactured industrial lights in aluminium, metal and bone china with distinctive design detailing such as colourful braided flexes/cables.

Skinflint design
skinflintdesign.co.uk
Original reclaimed and vintage lights salvaged from former industrial units across Europe and Russia. Plenty of Eastern Bloc factory lights to add a tough urban aesthetic to an interior. Range includes pendant shades, bulkheads, and fluorescent strip lights.

Urban Cottage Industries
urbancottageindustries.com
Bespoke Factorylux modular lighting parts to customize into individual styles, including cage lights, enamel pendant shades, bulkhead lanterns, ceiling roses, chain and braided flex/cable in a range of colours.

VINTAGE AND ARCHITECTURAL SALVAGE

Home Barn
homebarnshop.co.uk
Vintage industrial collectibles including furniture, lighting, accessories and signage.

LASSCO
lassco.co.uk
Architectural antiques, salvage, ex-industrial furniture and accessories as well as fixtures, fittings and materials.

Retrouvius
retrouvius.com
Reclamation and architectural salvage with a good range of ex-commercial and workplace tables, desks, seating, storage, signage and reclaimed timber.

KITCHENS AND BATHROOMS

Bert and May
bertandmay.com
Traditionally made encaustic floor and wall tiles, bespoke kitchens and bathrooms, concrete basins and a great range of brass fixtures with raw, beautiful finishes.

Holloways of Ludlow
hollowaysofludlow.com
Good source of architectural ironmongery, sanitary ware, lighting, cast-iron radiators and utilitarian kitchen fittings and accessories.

Nisbets
nisbets.co.uk
Commercial catering and canteen supplies: stainless-steel freestanding units, trolleys, bowls and accessories.

Plain English Design
plainenglishdesign.co.uk
Artisan-crafted kitchens with an utilitarian, old-fashioned scullery aesthetic. Industrial-inspired metal and glazed screens also available. UK & US studios.

WALLPAPERS, FABRICS AND TEXTILES

Deborah Bowness
deborahbowness.com
Charming trompe l'oeil *wallpaper designs hand-printed in the UK and including designs such as 'Genuine Fake Books', 'Utility Drawers' and 'New Cross Tiles'.*

Ian Mankin
ianmankin.co.uk
Traditional woven utility ticking, linen, indigo denim, gingham checks and canvas.

Sukha
atelier-sukha.nl
Independent lifestyle store stocking organic and ethical pieces for pared-down urban living, including wool and linen textiles, rustic daybeds and wooden stools, kitchenware and hand-thrown ceramics.

Puebco
Puebco.it
Great industrial and utility home decor, hardware and accessories, including metal canisters, canvas storage and army surplus-style textiles.

USA

FURNITURE AND ACCESSORIES

Canvas Home Store
canvashomestore.com
Simple furniture designs in natural wood and metal, relaxed linens, robust shelving and accessories that elegantly team form with function.

Home Stories
homestories.com
Brooklyn-based boutique offering a range of home furnishings in neutral and monochrome shades and with a pared-back aesthetic. Some utilitarian staples and natural textures that combine beauty, simplicity and authenticity.

Industrial Home
industrialhome.com
All styles of decor with a strong industrial reference for vintage, relaxed, bohemian and modern urban interiors.

West Elm
westelm.com
One-stop shop for classic urban essentials. Large sectional sofas in tweed, linen and wool, boho textiles, industrial glass jar lighting and utilitarian kitchen essentials all under one roof.

LIGHTING

Long Made Co.
Longmadeco.com
Custom-made industrial lighting in metal finishes including raw brass, polished nickel, steel, blackened brass and raw copper, ideal for adding a luxurious element to a bare brick backdrop.

Schoolhouse Electric
schoolhouseelectric.com
Extensive collection of iconic American industrial-inspired homewares that combine thoughtful living with good design, including utility kitchenware, factory clocks, tubular beds, drafting chairs and all styles of factory lighting.

Workstead
workstead.com
Elegant industrial-inspired wall, ceiling and floor fixtures in cast brass and black powder-coated brass and iron, beautifully combining function and flexibility.

WALLPAPER, FABRICS AND TEXTILES

Faribault Mill
faribaultmill.com
Classic blankets and woven textiles in heritage designs, including stripes, checks and plaids well as Army Medic, Navy and US cabin blankets.

NLXL
usa.nlxl.com
Dutch company producing striking trompe l'oeil *wallpaper in industrial finishes such as concrete, scrap wood, burnt wood and brick.*

KITCHENS AND BATHROOMS

American Restoration Tile
restorationtile.com
Modern reproductions of heritage industrial and commercial favourites including subway/metro brick tiles and encaustic styles.

March
marchsf.com
High-end furniture, cookware and serveware inspired by commercial kitchen and traditional pantry design. Classic utilitarian pieces, sturdy and well made.

Restoration Hardware
restorationhardware.com
Large range of bathroom furniture and fittings, including metal-wrapped industrial-style vanities and traditional clawfoot tubs.

VINTAGE AND ARCHITECTURAL SALVAGE

City Foundry
cityfoundry.com
Extensive range of industrial-influenced furniture, lighting and artefacts, including iconic classic mid-century pieces. Also CF Signature, a collection of industrial and mid-century modern-influenced pieces made to order.

Factory20
Factory20.com
Online stock of antique and vintage industrial furniture salvaged from factories, offices, commercial units and medical laboratories.

Three Potato Four
threepotatofourshop.com
Quirky collection of vintage industrial memorabilia and modern-day alternatives.

Salvage One
salvageone.com
Chicago-based treasure trove of rescued, recycled furniture, accessories and collectibles.

PICTURE CREDITS

All photography by Ben Edwards.
Key: **a** = above, **b** = below, **r** = right, **l** = left, **c** = centre

1 Interior by Marco Pasanella and Rebecca Robertson; **2** The London home of Peter Win; **3–4** The residence and studio of Jennifer and Liam Maher (aka Energy Plan Creative); **5al** Designer James van der Velden of Bricks Studio, Amsterdam; **5ac** Atelier Eiffel run by Isabelle Roque; **5ar** The New York home of Houssein Jarouche of MiCasa.com.br; **5bl** Atelier Eiffel run by Isabelle Roque; **5bc** Next Door's Space by Carin Scheve and Francesco Caramella; **5br** Atelier Eiffel run by Isabelle Roque; **6** The home of Louise Miller in London, available to hire through www.millerstyle.co.uk; **8–9** Designer James van der Velden of Bricks Studio, Amsterdam; **11al** Next Door's Space by Carin Scheve and Francesco Caramella; **11bl** Architecture and design by Manifold Architecture Studio, Brooklyn, NY; **11r** The canalside home and gallery of creative director, art dealer and location owner Mark Chalmers in Amsterdam, www.thegarageamsterdam.com and www.markchalmers.co; **12** Next Door's Space by Carin Scheve and Francesco Caramella; **13al** Designer James van der Velden of Bricks Studio, Amsterdam; **13ac** The New York home of Houssein Jarouche of MiCasa.com.br; **13b** Architecture & Design by Manifold Architecture Studio, Brooklyn, NY; **14** The residence and studio of Jennifer and Liam Maher (aka Energy Plan Creative); **15a** Designer James van der Velden of Bricks Studio, Amsterdam; **15bl** Next Door's Space by Carin Scheve and Francesco Caramella; **15br** The home of Louise Miller in London, available to hire through www.millerstyle.co.uk; **16ac** Interiors by Marco Pasanella and Rebecca Robertson; **16ar** The home of Anouk Pruim, Graphic Designer; **16b** The London home of Peter Win; **17** Designer James van der Velden of Bricks Studio, Amsterdam; **18l** Next Door's Space by Carin Scheve and Francesco Caramella; **18r** The canalside home and gallery of creative director, art dealer and location owner Mark Chalmers in Amsterdam, www.thegarageamsterdam.com and www.markchalmers.co; **19a** Atelier Eiffel run by Isabelle Roque; **19b** The London home of Peter Win; **20** Designer James van der Velden of Bricks Studio, Amsterdam; **21l** The home of Louise Miller in London, available to hire through www.millerstyle.co.uk; **21c** Designer James van der Velden of Bricks Studio, Amsterdam; **21r** The home of Louise Miller in London, available to hire through www.millerstyle.co.uk; **22al** Next Door's Space by Carin Scheve and Francesco Caramella; **22ar** The canalside home and gallery of creative director, art dealer and location owner Mark Chalmers in Amsterdam, www.thegarageamsterdam.com and www.markchalmers.co; **22bl** The home of Louise Miller in London, available to hire through www.millerstyle.co.uk; **22br** Next Door's Space by Carin Scheve and Francesco Caramella; **23** Designer James van der Velden of Bricks Studio, Amsterdam; **24l** The residence and studio of Jennifer and Liam Maher (aka Energy Plan Creative); **24r** The London home of Peter Win; **25l** The home of Louise Miller in London, available to hire through www.millerstyle.co.uk; **25r** Designer James van der Velden of Bricks Studio, Amsterdam; **26a and bl** The New York home of Houssein Jarouche of MiCasa.com.br; **25br** Atelier Eiffel run by Isabelle Roque; **26a** The residence and studio of Jennifer and Liam Maher (aka Energy Plan Creative); **26b** The home of Anouk Pruim, Graphic Designer;

28al Designer James van der Velden of Bricks Studio, Amsterdam; **28ac** The canalside home and gallery of creative director, art dealer and location owner Mark Chalmers in Amsterdam, www.thegarageamsterdam.com and www.markchalmers.co; **28ar and br** Designer James van der Velden of Bricks Studio, Amsterdam; **28bl** The residence and studio of Jennifer and Liam Maher (aka Energy Plan Creative); **28bc** Architecture & Design by Manifold Architecture Studio, Brooklyn, NY; **29** Designer James van der Velden of Bricks Studio, Amsterdam; **30** Interiors by Marco Pasanella and Rebecca Robertson; **31l and c** Designer James van der Velden of Bricks Studio, Amsterdam; **31r** Atelier Eiffel run by Isabelle Roque; **32–33** Interiors by Marco Pasanella and Rebecca Robertson; **34al and ac** Designer James van der Velden of Bricks Studio, Amsterdam; **34ar and ml** The canalside home and gallery of creative director, art dealer and location owner Mark Chalmers in Amsterdam, www.thegarageamsterdam.com and www.markchalmers.co; **34mc** Architecture & Design by Manifold Architecture Studio, Brooklyn, NY; **34mr and bl** The canalside home and gallery of creative director, art dealer and location owner Mark Chalmers in Amsterdam, www.thegarageamsterdam.com and www.markchalmers.co; **34bc and br** Atelier Eiffel run by Isabelle Roque; **35–45** Designer James van der Velden of Bricks Studio, Amsterdam; **46–53** Architecture & Design by Manifold Architecture Studio, Brooklyn, NY; **54–63** Atelier Eiffel run by Isabelle Roque; **64–75** The canalside home and gallery of creative director, art dealer and location owner Mark Chalmers in Amsterdam, www.thegarageamsterdam.com and www.markchalmers.co; **76al** The London home of Peter Win; **76ac** The New York home of Houssein Jarouche of MiCasa.com.br; **76ar** The residence and studio of Jennifer and Liam Maher (aka Energy Plan Creative); **76ml** Next Door's Space by Carin Scheve and Francesco Caramella; **76mc** The London home of Peter Win; **76mr** The New York home of Houssein Jarouche of MiCasa.com.br; **76bl and bc** Next Door's Space by Carin Scheve and Francesco Caramella; **76br** The London home of Peter Win; **77** The New York home of Houssein Jarouche of MiCasa.com.br; **78–87** Next Door's Space by Carin Scheve and Francesco Caramella; **88–95** The New York home of Houssein Jarouche of MiCasa.com.br; **96–105** The residence and studio of Jennifer and Liam Maher (aka Energy Plan Creative); **106–115** The London home of Peter Win; **116al** The home of Anouk Pruim, Graphic Designer; **116ac** Interiors by Marco Pasanella and Rebecca Robertson; **116ar** The home of Anouk Pruim, Graphic Designer; **116ml** The home of Louise Miller in London, available to hire through www.millerstyle.co.uk; **116mc** Designer James van der Velden of Bricks Studio, Amsterdam; **116mr** The home of Louise Miller in London, available to hire through www.millerstyle.co.uk; **116b and 117** The home of Anouk Pruim, Graphic Designer; **118–125** The home of Louise Miller in London, available to hire through www.millerstyle.co.uk; **126–135** The home of Anouk Pruim, Graphic Designer; **136–145** Interiors by Marco Pasanella and Rebecca Robertson; **146–153** Designer James van der Velden of Bricks Studio, Amsterdam; **157** The London home of Peter Win; **159** Architecture & Design by Manifold Architecture Studio, Brooklyn, NY; **160** Designer James van der Velden of Bricks Studio, Amsterdam.

BUSINESS CREDITS

Key: **a** = above, **b** = below, **r** = right, **l** = left, **c** = centre

Anouk Pruim Grafisch Ontwerp
www.anoukpruim.nl
Interiors: Brecht Murré
mekerwonen.nl
Architect: Joost de Haan
www.vvkh.nl
*Pages 16ar, 26 below, 116al,
116ar, 116b, 117, 126–135.*

Atelier Eiffel
Available to rent as an event
space and photographic location
and for business meetings.
www.ateliereiffel.com
*Pages 5ac, 5bl, 5br, 19 above,
25br, 31r, 34bc, 34br, 54–63.*

Bricks Studio
Lijnbaansgracht 119H
1016 VV Amsterdam
The Netherlands
T: + 31 (0)20 320 43 88
www.bricksstudio.nl
*Pages 5al, 8–9, 13al, 15a, 17,
20, 21c, 23, 25r, 28al, 28ar, 29,
31r, 31c, 34al, 34ac, 35–45,
116mc, 146–153, 160.*

Carin Scheve
Stylist
Carin Scheve's loft is available to
rent as a photographic location
and event space.
www.nextdoorsp.com
www.carinscheve.com
*Pages 5bc, 11al, 12, 15bl, 18l,
22al, 22 br, 76ml, 76bl, 76bc,
76bl, 76bc, 78–87.*

Jennifer Maher
Energy Plan Creative
www.energyplancreative.com
*Pages 3–4, 14, 24l, 26a, 28bl,
76ar, 96–105.*

Louise Miller
Interior stylist
www.millerstyle.co.uk
*Pages 6, 15br, 21l, 21r, 22bl,
25l, 116ml, 116mr, 118–125.*

Mark Chalmers
Creative director, art dealer
and location owner.
www.thegarageamsterdam.com
www.markchalmers.co
*Pages 11r, 18r, 22ar, 28ac,
34ar, 34ml, 34mr, 34bl, 64–75.*

Manifold.ArchitectureStudio
581 Myrtle Avenue
Brooklyn, NY 11205
United States
T: 001-347-223-5975
and
Luisenstrasse 27B
55124 Mainz
Germany
E: contact@mani-fold.com
www.mani-fold.com
*Pages 11bl, 13b, 28bc, 34mc,
46–53, 159.*

MiCasa
Rua Estados Unidos 2109
Jardim America
Sao Paulo
CEP 01427–002
Brazil
T: +55 11 3088 1238
www.MiCasa.com.br
*Pages 5ar, 13a, 26a, 26bl, 76a,
76mr, 77, 88–95.*

Peter Win
Peter Win's apartment is
available to hire as a
photographic location
E: winpeter@mac.com
*Pages 16b, 24r, 76mc,
106–115.*

Rebecca Robertson Interiors
www.rebeccarobertsoninteriors.
com
*Pages 1, 16ac, 30, 32, 33,
116ac, 136–145.*

INDEX

ACKNOWLEDGMENTS

Thank you to everyone at Ryland Peters & Small for the opportunity to work again with a publishing company that continues to invest in creating original content that makes for such a beautiful end result. Thank you particularly to my editor Annabel for calmly chivvying me along when faced with tight copy deadlines. And thank you, of course, to Ben, for taking photographs that capture the intrinsic beauty of each location.

    Huge gratitude also goes to all the homeowners for sharing so much of their creative ingenuity and passion for industrial interior living. Urban pioneering is as much about individual spirit and personality as it is about the buildings themselves. It's a refreshing new angle to a great subject matter, and I hope I've done it justice.

For my lovely Dad.